FRIENDSHIP IN ADOLESCENCE & YOUNG ADULTHOOD

FRIENDSHIP IN ADOLESCENCE & YOUNG ADULTHOOD

MOSHE SMILANSKY

Psychosocial & Educational Publications
Gaithersburg, Maryland

Copyright © 1991 Moshe Smilansky
All rights reserved. No part of this publication may be reproduced or distributed in any form or stored in a data base or retrieval system without the prior written permission of the publisher.

Printed in the United States of America

Published by:

Psychosocial & Educational Publications
P.O. Box 2146
Gaithersburg, Maryland 20886
301 869-4454

ISBN 0-9625963-5-3
Library of Congress Catalog Card Number: 90-72147

CONTENTS

Preface 7

Acknowledgements 11

Part I: Conceptual Framework
Introduction: The Importance of Friendship and Fellowship 13
1. The Challenge of Modernization
2. Friendship as Achievement

Chapter One: Understanding Friendship Development — 17
The Theory
1. Studies of Friendship: Description and Limitations
2. A Model for Understanding and Developing Friendship
   a. Basic Assumptions
   b. Contributing Factors

Chapter Two: Changes in the Perception of Friendship from 25
Childhood to Adolescence

Chapter Three: The Singular Import of Friendship During the 35
Adolescent Period
1. The Importance of Peer Groups
2. How a Peer Group Functions and Exerts Influence
3. Peer Group Activity: How it Serves the Individual
4. The Significance of Friends During Adolescence
5. Expectations of Friends

Chapter Four: The Development of Friendship During 51
Adolescence
1. Shaping Identity through Peers and Friends
2. Stages of Friendship
3. The Need for a Variety of Potential Friends
4. Difficulties and Conflict in Friendship
5. Differences in Friendship Patterns: Boys and Girls

Chapter Five: Social Organizations: Their Influence on the 79
Development of Friendship
1. Geographic Proximity
2. Organizational and Structural Factors
3. The School's Social and Educational Climate

Chapter Six: Loneliness 85
1. The Scope of the Problem
2. The Causes of Loneliness: The Processes and their
   Significance
3. Children without Friends
4. Loneliness for Adolescents

Bibliography 97

Part II: Suggested Group Experiences
   A. Getting Acquainted and Cohesion in Social Groups   105
   Introduction
    1. Getting Acquainted for the First Time
    2. Deeper Acquaintance
    3. Readiness for Initiation — Getting Acquainted
    4. What is a Group?
    5. The Significance of the Social Group
    6. The Contribution of the Group in Various Coping Strategies
    7. Creating a Relaxed Atmosphere in the Group
    8. Openness in the Group
    9. "The Gift of Happiness"
   10. Constructive Criticism
   11. Asking the Group for Help
   12. Developing Communication Skills
   13. Attention to Verbal and Non-Verbal Communication
   14. Expressing Emotion
   15. Communication and Cooperation
   16. Speaking and Listening
   17. Work-Style in a Social Group
   B. Friendship   141
   Introduction
    1. What is "Friendship"?
    2. Friendship at Different Ages
    3. Criteria for Choosing a Friend
    4. Characteristics of a Friend and their Contribution within the Friendship Process
    5. Personal Characteristics and their Contribution to the Friendship Process
    6. Qualities and Behavior which damage the Friendship Process
    7. Ups and Downs of Relationships
    8. The Expectations Gap Between Friends
    9. Conflicts within Friendship
   10. Revealing Secrets
   11. Tale-bearing and Trustworthiness
   12. Insults, Competition and Jealousy
   13. The Third One in a Friendship Group
   14. Anger and Ending Friendship
   15. Loneliness
   16. Making New Friends
   17. Accepting Differences within Friendship
   18. Concluding Meeting

Preface

The series **The Challenge of Adolescence** is aimed at the various professional staff-educators, teachers, counselors, psychologists, social workers, youth leaders-involved in the educational system and who come into contact with adolescents. It offers a detailed program, based on an educational psycho-social approach, for guiding a special type of peer group structure

The purpose of the program is to help the adolescent cope with the challenge involved in undergoing adolescence in a modern democratic society.

A modern democratic society presents a difficult challenge to adolescence. In traditional society answers to questions of personal identity and social responsibility were provided by religion, community, family and/or the ruling authority. In modern society the individual feels free to examine various options available and determine for himself what his life will be like. Moreover, the context within which the adolescent must search for the answers to his questions of personal identity is undergoing tremendous, often radical change during the very period of search.

The transitional phase of his life, adolescence, has been extended (ages 11-21) and has attained new and vital significance. It is during this time that the adolescent may face the difficult questions which face him no matter which way he turns: "Who am I?" "What are my capabilities?" "How can I make friends?" "With whom should I make friends?" "What does the future hold for me?" "What sort of life-style should I adopt?" "What shall I BE? What sort of career should I take up?" "What sort of relationship should I aim for with my parents?" "What role shall I play in the society in which I live?"

The adolescent needs systematic support in developing his ego, shaping his personal identity, and in fostering an ability to cope and to accept social responsibility.

Schools may answer these needs. They do not only provide the adolescent with a certain level of knowledge and skills in various subjects, but may also provide environments within which the student may develop mature personal and interpersonal functioning. Such curricula need be based on cognitive and affective approaches to the learning situation. The peer group, already playing an important role in the life of the adolescent, can provide an important element in this process. Learning through group experience can encourage personal involvement and commitment while promoting self-knowledge and developing new patterns of behavior.

The series consists of a structured, systematic program geared to the needs of adolescents. It includes six volumes, each focusing on a significant area in the life of adolescents.

Volume 1: Getting Acquainted, Social Groups and Friendship

Volume 2: Boys and Girls: Forming a Sexual Identity and Relations with the Opposite Sex

Volume 3: Between Adolescents and Parents

Volume 4: What am I Going to Be when I Grow Up? Identifying and developing a future career.

Volume 5: Stress and Pressure in Adolescence (including coping with alcohol, drugs and suicide)

Volume 6: Moving Into the Future (including self evaluation, choosing a mate, preparing to enter a career)

The Challenge of Adolescence on the Threshold of the 21st Century presents the theoretical background to our approach in this series (Smilansky, 1990). The book broadens the horizons of those who wish to implement the series and explains the principles of organizing and guiding a supportive peer group to group leaders.

Each volume in the series is divided into two parts. Part One provides theoretical material and items of interest to the group facilitators. Part Two describes group experiences, adapted to work in peer groups according to the principles of the approach elaborated in the book mentioned above.

Each volume in the series, as well as the group experiences described within, form an independent unit. Facilitators may, therefore, choose the subjects on which the group will work according to various factors: the personal qualities of the facilitator (personal values, experience in group dynamics, etc.), the group composition (sex mix, age, level of maturity, etc.), the organizational framework (school, religious institution, community center, etc.).

The program has been carried out for several years and has been revised in accordance with feedback received from the group leaders. We would appreciate receiving comments and suggestions arising from your use of the materials included in the series, to be considered in preparing the second edition of the series.

Volume I of the series deals with Getting Acquainted and Friendship. Fellowship and friendship denote an interpersonal relationship based on equality and reciprocity. They are significant to all people and at every age. However, friendship develops more intensively in the period of adolescence than at any other age. Successful friendship experience will give the adolescent confidence in his ability to engage in intimate, honest and reciprocal interpersonal relationships throughout his life.

Acknowledgements

This book was prepared on the foundation of two research and curriculum development projects: the first in the Israeli Unit for Research and Curriculum Development of the Tel-Aviv University School of Education (supported by the Division for Curriculum Development in the Ministry of Education and Culture); and the second in the United States Job Corps, of the U.S. Federal Government, Department of Labor.

Both projects were field-based experiments of such proportions that it could not have been accomplished without the assistance and goodwill of literally hundreds of people. Their magnitude precludes our mentioning every person who contributed to the research, field experiments, training of personnel, typing and retyping, editing, etc. The outcome is a synergistic result of all their efforts.

We will only mention the composition of the teams that prepared the experimental learning exercises: Moshe Smilansky, Professor, Chairperson and Project Head; Shoshana Feldman, M.A., career development psychologist, Coordinator; Michal Roseman, M.A., child clinical psychologist; Rachel Zorman, Ph.D., educational psychologist; Sarah Smilansky, Professor of child clinical psychology; Alina Sheleks, M.A. child clinical psychologist; Rachel Weiser, counseling specialist. English language editors: Shoshana Rotschild and Karen Abramovitz.

Introduction: The Importance of Friendship and Fellowship

1. The Challenge of Modernization

The subject of fellowship and friendship has occupied philosophers, sociologists, poets and writers for generations. However, recent psychological and sociological research has given it new and vital significance. Various social phenomena, whose causes and patterns are described in the book, **The Challenge of Adolescence on the Threshold of the 21st Century** by M. Smilansky, have made it necessary to ensure that the adolescent in our society will understand the significance of the need to take an active role in maintaining fellowship and friendship. Demographic changes, changes in role patterns and modes of functioning within the community, the family, the school and other institutions have made it necessary for children as well as adults to learn and relearn, if necessary, how to face the necessity of severing relations with people with whom they were close. They must learn to construct friendships with a variety of people, to form a number of friendly relationships and develop friendships which will meet their new and changing needs.

Changes in the community structure or moving to a new community require the establishment of new interpersonal relationships. Entering a new community, or switching from a private to a public school within one's old community, disrupts the pupil's social circle and requires an adjustment to a new peer group, consisting of unfamiliar personalities as well as unfamiliar stereotypical features which may interfere with the process of forming new relationships.

Upon leaving school the individual must carry out his plans for the future. He finds himself responsible for his own activities and that his success or failure is often inextricably linked to his doing or not doing what is necessary. He must adjust to social and intellectual expectations of his roommates or classmates at college or university; he must respond adequately to bosses and fellow workers in the place he works;

he must take the steps necessary for him to reach the goal he has set for himself.

As times have changed, the family which had been the bulwarks against isolation and loneliness, has become the site of such loneliness: both parents work and the children come home to empty houses; smaller and smaller families have made single child families common; or if two children, they are close together in age, competing for the same roles and often for the same space within the family; broken communication between parents and children leave both sides silent and dumb; divorces produce parents who won't speak to each other, who live on opposite ends of the earth, whose children are torn between factions within the family; changing life-styles has produced single-parent families where the parent chooses to bring up his/her child despite being alone. In the quest for career marriage is postponed, children leave home and move from apartment to apartment, often sharing it with strangers, and the high rate of divorce, a sort of serial monogamy, means that friendship formation processes may be repeated many times in a relatively short period of time.

Older, more settled people, turn to their friends to help them cope with pressures of family life and work. Upon retirement or the loss of a spouse, especially with the expectation of a long life still stretching ahead, the fear of loneliness and need for the support of friends grow greater. Forming new friendships is vital to social and emotional adjustment in all stages of life.

2. Friendship as Achievement

Learning to make and keep friends means achievement in three areas:

* The immediate sense of gratification arising from the mutual investment of friends in each other. The significance of this changes from one age to another, and may differ between boys and girls. However, at each stage of development fellowship and friendship help the adolescent acquire a sense of confidence in his self estimation and his ability to cope; he enriches his experiential life, moves ahead in the process of differentiating from his parents and becomes better able to formulate a personal identity.

* The ability to establish and maintain significant, long term interpersonal relationships in various areas and with different people as the result of having attained a high "social IQ"-social perception plus social skills-in the area of fellowship and friendship.
* Successful experiences with regard to a variety of friends and acquaintances will lead to a process of preventive as well as promotive learning during adolescence. Repeated positive experiences in this sphere affects learning holistically which in turn provides the learner with confidence in his ability to engage in intimate, honest and reciprocal interpersonal transactions for the rest of his life. Each time this achievement is repeated, he confirms his ability to do so. The sense of this achievement serves as protection from the fear of loneliness which faces a large portion of the population in modern society.

Although fellowship and friendship make up a single area of activity in the broader, unlimited sphere of social development and interpersonal relations with which the entire program deals, this area is considered basic to all the others in the development of social skills, and group leaders and facilitators are enjoined to keep that in mind when making their choice of what to deal with first.

Chapter One: Understanding Friendship Development-The Theory

1. Studies of Friendship: Description and Limitations

Psychological and sociological writings reflected an interest in the subject of friendship as early as the beginning of this century. Harry S. Sullivan, the noted psychologist (1953), considered developing interpersonal relations to be central to his theory of the development of the personality. Basing his conclusions on his personal experience of loneliness, he maintained that friendship is a vital and significant topic in the periods of preadolescence and early adolescence, as will be detailed further.

The interest in friendship peaked in the past decade and research from the 1980's has contributed to five aspects of understanding friendship:
* the development in the perception of the term "friendship"
* the process through which children and adolescents develop friendships
* the influence of schools and other societal institutions on friendship patterns
* the implications of the absence of friendship (loneliness)
* the effect of supportive intervention on promoting development of friendship skills

It is, in our opinion, vital that such information be made available to all those working in fields having to do with adolescents. It is, however, important to note that there are problems and limitations to be considered when looking at the results of the various studies, such as limitations in theoretical terms, samples studied, research tools used, etc. Our presentation will deal with these problems initially and then go on to discuss generalizations which seem to be important. Following the generalizations, we shall present specific findings concerning the various stages and elements of human development in the subject under discussion.

The principal limitation seems to be in the area of theory. Allen (1981), for example, summarizes his view as a developmental psychologist that "examination of the research on friendship among children leads to the conclusion that theory in this field is not sufficiently developed, and that the efforts devoted to theoretical work have been too few." (p. 195) He adds that one of the principal theoretical limitations has to do with the question of development; he asks "to what extent the psychological processes on which social relations are based differ at different points of development throughout life"? (p. 196) It would seem that we need a developmental theory in this field.

The second limitation becomes clear upon examining field studies: how they are conducted and their scope. Gottman (1981) asks: "Why do certain children develop friendships, while others don't? Since the process of friendship formation has not been sufficiently researched, we are not able to give a direct answer to this question." Both Gottman and his critics agree that we still have a long way to go in establishing a theory, creating reliable research tools and validating various samples, in which the roles of age, sex, social background and ecological system are understood.

Adelson and Doehrman (1980) point up the third limitation which has to do specifically with the subject of our interest in this program. "Friendship, whose significance is so great in the life of the adolescent-both in its presence and in its absence-remains a subject essentially unresearched by psychologists." (p. 107)

Nevertheless, despite these limitations, it is possible to distinguish what seems significant, particularly in view of the importance of friendship, from the various studies. The studies quoted are from various disciplines: the schools of psychology, including developmental, social, educational and clinical; aspects of sociology including structural, phenomenological and anthropological; and other behavioral sciences including that of communication which have dealt with the subject of fellowship and friendship, albeit from their individual points of view.

The studies represent a variety of approaches. Some concentrated on understanding the development of the concept of friendship over a period of time, focusing on the development of a social perspective. Others focused on particular ages, such as early childhood, and observed social behavior including interpersonal social relationships defined as friendships. Sociologists concentrated on the social organization called "school" in order to understand further the process by which the organization and function of schools affects social development.

The results of our study may serve as a theoretical background for educational approaches of counselors, educators and all others interested in promoting adolescent psycho-social development. Therefore, we will begin, in the next section, by presenting the basic assumptions underlying the comprehensive theoretical model we have developed with regard to our general approach. Then, we will present significant contributions from various areas of research.

2. A Model for Understanding and Developing Friendship
A. Basic Assumptions

The Challenge of Adolescence on the Threshold of the 21st Century discusses our comprehensive approach in detail. However, here, we shall present some of the basic assumptions significant to understanding the subject of this volume: fellowship and friendship.

1. Friendship and fellowship is a universal aspect of human and social development which occurs throughout life. Modernization has meant that friendship and fellowship has assumed a unique and vital significance and has developed according to new and different patterns. It can be defined as the interpersonal relationship based on equality and reciprocity and maintains its significance from early childhood to old age.

2. Clinical experience and studies in developmental psychology have indicated that there is a developmental hierarchy of social perception of the concept of friendship which varies according to level of maturation and according to the significance of the experience of friendship.

3. Psychoanalysts, joined later by psychologists and sociologists, saw fellowship and friendship as vital, particularly during the later stages of adolescence, in establishing individuations differentiation from the family in general and from parents in particular. This in turn led to the formation of a personal identity.

4. Sociologists and social psychologists described ecological systems which included expressions of the ethos of different cultures, institu-

tional organization and learning patterns and their effects on the differential development of needs in friendship and on the social behavior of both children and adults. One ecological system, the school, has a tremendous, often crucial, effect on formation and cessation of friendships. It is, therefore, of ultimate import for school principals, counselors and classroom teachers to understand how they work.

5. Phenomenological social psychologists and sociologists have shown how a person's perception of his position within a group of friends or colleagues has a tremendous, sometimes crucial, effect on his behavior. Differences in reaction patterns of both adults and children often stem from differences in their subjective perception of a situation rather than on what are the "objective" facts.

6. Psychologists and social psychologists have shown how the human being, from childhood on, plays an active role in fulfilling his own needs, in shaping his identity and in his ability to cope. This activity can be seen in observing child development, child-parent relations, pupil-teacher relations and friendship relations. Although there are many outside factors influencing the process of maturation, ultimately it is the young person who must struggle for individuation and shape his own life.

7. General activity referred to above takes on different significance at different maturation stages, depending on the needs of the individual and on the tasks society sets. The central task is to form a personal identity. This complex process is complicated by the uniqueness of the individual which has reached that stage of development and by the nature of the modern social institutions which intervene in the process: the nuclear family, school, post-high school institutions of learning, work, the army and religious institutions, for those who encounter them. The adolescent must cope with the tasks of differentiation from parents, social adjustment, individuation and social integration while moving through the influences of these various socializing frameworks. Forming friendships, concluding friendships, attempting friendships with other adolescents are partly unconscious and partly conscious activities. Such activities lead to the fulfillment of needs while gradually fashioning a profile of personal identity and at the same time serve the affective and cognitive needs of the present.

8. More recently clinical psychologists, psychiatrists, social psychologists and sociologists have dealt with the effects of loneliness. Loneliness has always existed, but with modernization, it has become more extensive. Parents, therapists and educators are all familiar with the suffering of children, adolescents, and adults who have no friends and are on the fringes of their class, their peer group or other social grouping. Modernization with its influence on the modes of institutional activity and the concomitant rise in the individual's expectations of self-fulfillment have both contributed to great difficulties in interpersonal transaction and increased the sense of loneliness. There seems to be a connection between shyness and loneliness in childhood and adolescence and social failure and loneliness in later life.

9. An ideology believing in a social responsibility to act on behalf of the individual plus accumulating evidence that the promotion of social skills and competence in making and keeping friends has positive results in childhood and adolescence are the bases for our activities in supportive intervention. We believe that fellowship and friendship can be learned within a social context, which we call a "Positive Peer Support" Group (PPS), and wish to make it possible for every adolescent to develop the social IQ necessary for making and maintaining fellowship and friendship. The concept of social IQ includes a high level of sensitivity to the socially significant, the skill of forming friendships and maintaining them as long as they are mutually meaningful, and of being able to conclude relationships in a positive manner when it becomes necessary to do so. Some adolescents achieve this level on their own. Others, however, need support. It is the responsibility of the facilitator to make sure that there is no group member who feels loneliness as a "natural" result of modern life. In our view this is a vital part of the development of basic skills in adolescents. Just as schools are responsible for ensuring their students attain proficiency in reading and arithmetic, so too with social IQ, including the area of friendship.

The above assumptions, as well as others detailed in our book, have led us to establish a systematic approach involving a systematic program of situation-oriented activities which promote development and change within the participants and which are related to each of the activity-spheres described in this series, including the area of friendship. Thus, when we discuss the development of fellowship and friendship, we must view each of the basic assumptions mentioned above as one factor within a complex of elements affecting readiness for and competence in developing fellowship and friendship. It is not possible to look at the basic attributes of one or another individual and ignore the influence of other factors which have a combined effect on that individual's present and future development. Although we are aware of the role played by personalities and needs of people in the process of developing a mutual relationship, we are also aware of a whole array of other factors which are also involved: the past, the present and the projected future. The combination of these factors affects the pattern of interpersonal and group transactions and produces a unique mode of life.

Fellowship and friendship in adolescence develop as two-way mutual obligations within the framework of broader relationships, such as members of the same class, members of a sports team, members of a youth group, members of a neighborhood group. Many significant questions arise with regard to such a situation. For example, what is the effect of such a friendship on the overall peer group and what is the effect of the peer group on friendship patterns? What is the effect of the development of heterosexual relationships on unisex friendships? What is the difference between friends from class and friends from the youth group? or friends from class and friends made in the dormitory of a boarding school? or friends from the dormitory of a boarding school compared with friends made in a dormitory of a non-educational institution?

B. Contributing Factors

Six principal factors combine in affecting developments in the sphere of friendship:

1. The cultural patterns of the society or group — at a given time and in a given cultural and social system. Part of this influence can be defined in terms of the inclusive superior powers of cultural ethos; part can be defined in terms of normative definitions of sexual roles (values, motives, attitudes and behavior) which are expressed in dress, speech, gestures, social behavior, courtship, recreation and other activities.

2. The developmental attributes of the individual — the biography and the given state of the individual, who has undergone a developing process of experience and personality formation. Several attributes may be mentioned as examples: body-build and physical self-image, competence and fitness, self image and self esteem, sexual identity and perception of sexual role, locus of control, motives for achievement in general and achievement in social relationships in particular, values and attitudes toward interpersonal in general and toward relationships between the sexes in particular, and social skills-competence in interpersonal relationships in general and in friendship in particular.

3. The influence of the family — actively exerting influence in various ways, some of them conscious and some unconscious. This includes transmitting qualities through socialization; maintaining values, expectations and norms of behavior; maintaining interpersonal relations at a certain level-among members of the family, between each of the members and his friends, and between the family as a unit and its friends and relatives; certain modes of behavior-direct and indirect-towards friends and acquaintances whom the child brings home or with whom the child has transactions outside the home.

4. The organization and activity of social institutions — first and foremost including the school: the kind of school, its social composition; the level of the groupings; whether or not the child is included in selective projects; the social climate-cooperative or competitive; the self image of the school as a whole; all these affect the patterns of friendship and selection of friends during adolescence and afterwards.

5. Stages and patterns in developing social perspective — the changes of the perception of the concept of friendship from childhood to and throughout adolescence, based on evidence from developmental studies and direct testimony. The crucial factor is age, but there are also differences in the definition of expectations, needs and response patterns based on sex. In addition, there are individual differences in the rate and pattern of development. These changes are a function of the development of social cognition (parallel to or following the development of general cognition and moral judgment), and are partly influenced by maturation tasks-the social tasks of the particular stage in maturation.

6. Various influences in a given ecological system — man is an active agent who shapes and is shaped, who forms interpersonal attachments and changes them at every stage of his development. Moreover, at any given time the individual acts simultaneously in various social systems- in the neighborhood, in the classroom, in a youth group, in a sports team, etc. Acquaintance relationships, sometimes intimate friendships, develop in each of these systems. In this model the patterns of transaction and the influence of activity in various systems represent the **horizontal** dimension in the development of friendship, while the previous point dealt with the influence of the **vertical** dimension.

Considering the significance of these contributing factors to the development of the adolescent, we shall now present scientific evidence, psycho-social assumptions and our pedagogical commentary with regard to the area at hand.

Chapter Two: Changes in the Perception of Friendship From Childhood to Adolescence

Friendship exists at all ages, but its attributes-cognitive, emotional and social-differ with age. With young children friendship is based on a sense of partnership which focuses on objects and shared activities, while with adolescents there is a pronounced expectation of a deep, effective reciprocity, based on a high level of social perspective, on commitment to intimacy, on mutual authenticity in communication and on mutual support which is not contingent upon agreement on any given subject. It is possible to say, in general, that as children develop, they grow in their capacity to attain a higher level of social IQ. They are able

* to perceive themselves and others as human beings-that each person has his own biographical past and his own needs and problems in the present (in the various ecological systems like school, family, peer group, team, etc.) and his own dreams for shaping his life in the future.
* to understand their own feelings and those of others; to free themselves of the egocentricity characterizing childhood and the beginning of adolescence; to exhibit a higher level of empathy for the emotional significance of various social situations in which others find themselves; and basing their attitude towards others on insights into the roles and situations of the others rather than on their own vantage point.
* to show readiness and competence for interpersonal interaction, the capacity to show understanding, to reveal themselves and share their deepest feelings.

Friendships in later adolescence are, therefore, more resistant to situational conflicts, more stable, richer and more consistent when compared with those of childhood and early adolescence.

In Selman's study (1980) we find a clear and systematic formulation of the developmental hierarchy of the perception of the concept of friendship. The following scale is based on his work with the addition of evidence from other research in the field. Selman's study focused on the development of social perspective. He interviewed about 100 subjects, aged 4-34 and defined five developmental levels. He also cited the ages at which a certain level of insight may be expected. It must be noted that his scale of development shows some overlapping in age levels due to individual differences.

Level 0-Egocentric and Undifferentiated (Ages 3-6). The child identifies social closeness with spatial proximity. For instance, the child perceives a "close friend" to be someone who lives close by, with whom he plays. Friendship is shared play activity and a friend is a playmate. Problems of envy or the intervention of a third party in the game are defined in terms of specific conflicts over the use of a toy or play-space rather than as conflicts involving development of personal or interpersonal feelings.

Level 1-Subjective or Differential (Ages 5-9). The child understands that even when social conditions are perceived to be equal or similar, different children may perceive things, in terms of themselves and others, in different ways. At this stage of development the child realizes the inherent uniqueness of each individual's psychological profile. His perception of friendship involves unilateral help. That means a friend is important insofar as he or she performs activities vital to the child. What is important is the approach of a person without any consideration of the implications for the other's needs. A good friend is someone who knows his likes and dislikes well and fulfills his needs better than anyone else.

Level 2-Self-reflective Perspective (Ages 7-12). At this age children are capable of examining their feelings and thoughts from the vantage point of another person's perspective. That means they are capable of putting themselves in the "shoes" of the other person and viewing themselves as the other person might perceive them. This new insight into the relationship between their view of themselves and that of another person's perspective allows them to compare their concepts and evaluations with those of others with whom they interact. Thus, they become aware of new forms of reciprocity within an interpersonal context.

This stage of relationship is predicated on an awareness of mutuality as part of relationships. An understanding of the two-way quality to the interaction means recognition of the need to coordinate expectations and mutual adaptation as opposed to the former expectation that the other would adapt his activity to one's fixed norms.

At this stage there is still a lack of continuity in expectation of mutuality. Thus, an argument on any matter may lead to a break-up of the friendship, although the feelings of the friend still exist.

This means that there is, as yet, no willingness to continue the friendship, although the feelings for the friend still exist. That is why Selman named this stage of the perception of friendship: "Fair Weather Friendships."

Level 3-"The Third Person" or The Stage of Mutual Perspective (Ages 10-15). The individual is aware of the potential for change within interpersonal relationships. As the result of the influence of various perspectives, the individual moves to a higher level of considering the needs of others and a willingness to relinquish the two-directional interaction perspective and become a "third party", viewing the needs and reactions of the two people involved from the outside. The capacity to adopt a third-party perspective helps the individual to develop an awareness of the complexity of mutuality within interpersonal relationships, in theory and in practice.

At this point the individual becomes aware of the significance of continuity in relationships and the nature of the bond between close friends. Friendship is no longer perceived simply as a solution to the problem of boredom and loneliness, but rather as a basic means of developing mutual intimacy and continuing support. At this point friends will share personal problems with each other and continue to be friends despite conflicts which may arise.

The emphasis on pair-commitment, characteristic of this stage, can lead to a feeling of domination and emotional suffocation. A closed relationship of this type may gradually lead many children to the conclusions that it is difficult to establish and maintain such relationships for a long period of time.

We can summarize this level as including the following perceptions:
* conflicts may develop due to differences in traits of the friends
* conflicts of certain types may strengthen the friendship in the long run rather than weaken or end it
* the difference between superficial conflicts and fundamental conflicts as well as the perception of alternative ways of dealing with conflict

According to Selman, discussion and clarification of problems can be a suitable way of solving them when differences in perception of a situation or behavioral reactions are revealed.

Level 4--The Societal or In-Depth Perspective (Ages 12-maturity). The individual is ready for subjective conceptualizing of interpersonal relationships in terms of mutuality which is no longer solely bilateral. The multidimensional complexities accommodated in such relationships express themselves in a depth of feeling and communication. The individual develops the capacity to perceive multifaceted relationships with different people. With some of them he will develop superficial relations involving the exchange of information and from whom he may expect a reaction on the level of mutual interest; with others he will attain a level of understanding and a depth of feeling which cannot be expressed.

In addition, systematic interpersonal perspectives develop which take into account the personalities of those involved, their situation and problems, and the ecological system within which they function. These perspectives are also generalized into a differential perception of universal responsibility, legal responsibility or moral responsibility. We are now dealing with friendship which combines personal autonomy with mutual interdependence.

The concept of mutual interdependence at this stage develops into the perception that friendship may be translated into the readiness of the individual to be autonomous and mutually committed at the same time. The autonomy is manifested in each of the friends accepting the need of the other to form meaningful relationships with others and to develop through such experiences.

The dependence, on the other hand, is manifested in each of the friend's feeling that he can depend on the support of the other, in both drawing strength from each other and gaining a sense of personal identity by means of identification with an other; a meaningful person with whom the relationship of friendship is unique and different from other friendships with people for whom the relationship may be different and, in certain aspects, less significant.

The way people who have reached Level 4 think illustrates how the development of social cognition aids the adolescent to develop the capacity for more complex understanding in all areas of interpersonal transaction.

Such capacity leads to understanding how internal personality conflicts of individuals within a friendship can affect the emergence of conflicts between the friends. This includes a realization of the advisability not to block communication paths during a crisis period, and to express sensitivity toward the deeper aspects of the feelings between oneself and one's friend through showing interest, providing feedback and support, etc. Furthermore, the individual is aware that activities of a certain nature could signal a willingness to solve the conflict within the relationship. As Selman indicated in his definition of the hierarchical stages of development, a broader, more profound understanding of the complexity of the situation arises from insights gained in previous stages which have been transferred to the next level. Selman's studies (Selman, 1981) show that in most cases there is no regression. A child who has discovered the importance of mutuality in friendship will not forget that principle and will understand other interpersonal situations in the light of his developing insight. It must, of course, be mentioned that the capacity for high level perception does not ensure the social skill and emotional readiness required for a relationship that is desirable from the standpoint of the expectations of all those involved.

Gottman (1981) studied the development of friendship in children aged 3-9 and noted five criteria which define the development process of childhood friendship.

1. The effective exchange of information
2. The ability to find areas in common and similarities between oneself and another
3. Finding effective solutions to interpersonal conflicts
4. Establishing a tie which is characterized by positive reciprocity
5. Willingness for risk-taking self-disclosure and interpersonal emptional exchange

Studies have shown that children do indeed improve with age in all five of the above criteria. Gottman maintains that this improvement is related to the general cognitive development of the child.

In studies conducted in Scotland Bigelow (1977) found that six year old children describe friendship as shared activities, not mentioning behavior relating to systematic commitment or mutuality, while 12 year olds included concepts of loyalty and mutual commitment as part of the fundamental definition of friendship..Bigelow defined three stages of development in the concept of friendship:

Stage One: friendship is conceived of as common activity between peers or neighbors who like one another more than others at least for that specific period of time.

Stage Two: friendship now includes mutual esteem and a sense of the need for this special relationship to continue.

Stage Three: friendship now includes expectations of mutual acceptance, mutual responsibility and commitment, honesty, self-disclosure and mutual intimacy.

A joint study by Bigelow and La Gaipa, based on the testimony of school children in Canada and Scotland (Bigelow & La Gaipa, 1980) notes the following:

In the middle grades of elementary school, the main expectation of friendship focuses around a positive opinion of the friend and on shared activities. A "positive opinion" means being "nice" and "considerate," general descriptive terms. Friendship development is described as shared activities which provide emotional support, i.e., ego reinforcement by the friend. Breaking off a friendship is described in terms of conflicts, i.e., the friend causing injury to the ego.

In adolescents, loyalty and commitment have become vital elements of a "best friend." Breaking off a friendship at this stage is described in terms of lack of loyalty and an ill opinion of a friend is expressed in terms of a moral deficiency of his character.

During the adolescent period (age 13-17) there is a declining emphasis on the friend being "nice" and supportive and a growing value on his loyalty. Intimacy becomes more important (16% for 13 year olds and 50% for 17 year olds). Honesty is cited as a factor important for developing friendship and the lack of honesty is a cause for its decline and break-up. Adolescents seek loyal friends who can be depended upon in difficult situations, particularly during "emotional crises." Bigelow and La Gaipa note that there is no substantial difference during childhood between actual friendship and ideal friendship. Adolescents, on the other hand, make more of a distinction between the ideal friend and the real friend. These findings are compatible with Piaget's theory that the concept of the ideal is a unique quality characteristic of the transition to formal thinking, which is characteristic of adolescent development (Inhelder and Piaget, 1958). According to Bigelow and La Gaipa the difference between the ideal and the actual can be explained by the fact that many adolescents lack the social skill for interpersonal relationships which is necessary for realizing their ideals.

The theory of social exchange can explain the variables necessary for the development of friendship: intimacy and mutual support. Thus, an exchange of intimate information, emotional support and pleasure in shared activity can result in the development of friendship. However, the cessation of friendship does not seem to involve simply a disruption of social exchange (fewer than one percent noted that "he stopped helping me" or "she stopped sharing intimate things with me" etc.), but rather is attributed to such qualities as a lack of loyalty, falseness (inauthenticity), or moral lacks. It would seem that the breaking off of a friendship during this period involves attaching a negative label to the erstwhile friend rather than simply noting the absence of good qualities or of mutuality. Therefore, we would explain the cessation of friendship by means of the attribution theory rather than that of social exchange.

The search for patterns manifests itself in sensitivity to the significance of various terms used by the subjects in their own free-form descriptions. Thus, we see in Bigelow and La Gaipa's story of a boy describing the breakup of his friendship: "After we broke up, he started telling everybody lies about me and so did his new friends." This example shows the characteristics of attributing a negative label rather than simply noting the need to break off the friendship, it indicates the new loyalty of the ex-friend to his new group, and it also illustrates the conflict between pair friendships and the dependency of clique membership.[1]

Values and expectations involved in the development of friendship also change in the transition from childhood to adolescence. In childhood, at the age of nine for example, a child's expectations are clear. He expects his friend to be kind and courteous, to share experiences, and, especially, not to have aggressive intentions. Some children at this age also judge their friends by the way in which they treat other children: "Someone you can play with and have fun with; who cares what happens to you; who is ready to give you things that belong to him; who won't hit you; and who will show you mutual respect."

In early adolescence, at the age of 13, we see a wide range of expectations, indicating the transition into adolescence: answers range from those of moral judgment, characteristic of childhood, to those of loyalty and honesty, characteristic of later adolescence.

In late adolescence we find expectations of friendship similar to those of early adolescence, but with a greater emphasis on loyalty and confidentiality and also a growing awareness of the role of friendship in personal social development as well as a more realistic perception of the function of friendship. The following statement illustrates this: close friends are essential because we need someone "who knows us better than we know ourselves. A friend does not always have to be with you when you need him, because in reality that is not always possible..."

Youniss conducted interviews inquiring about friendship (Youniss, 1980). He asked his subjects to define friendship and to describe how friendship is initiated, maintained and broken off. Youniss also found that the concepts of mutual understanding and intimacy become central in friendship in adolescence. Understanding to the adolescent means conceiving the other, the friend, as someone who has his own abilities and experiences. The individual's involvement in the conception of the other is parallel to his/her expectation that the friend show interest in his/her personality and a similar understanding. The development of this understanding leads to a differential choice of friends,

---

1 "Clique" is used to refer to a group of 4-5 adolescent friends; it is characterized by a high degree of involvement and cohesion. "Gang" refers to a band of 10-15 youths who hang out together, on the streets or in accepted gathering spots, and who do things together as a group, such as go to the movies, to the beach or bowling, etc.

friends who will understand one and respond to one's needs. Compatibility is sought between two different, complex and unique entities. Intimacy, according to Youniss, is manifested in two interrelated ways:

1. Friendship provides an opportunity for self-disclosure; with a friend it is possible to share one's feelings and opinions quite frankly.

2. A friend can be trusted; you can rely on a friend not to use what you have revealed to him or what he knows about you against you.

Summary of the Development of the Concept of Friendship. The following points can be summarized from the material discussed by various researchers, and from interviews that we conducted:

* The concept of friendship is a vital component in the development of a social IQ, which provides the adolescent and the adult with an understanding of himself and of others, an understanding of the processes of interpersonal transaction, the possibility of accepting support and gaining a sense of security and the capacity to cope successfully in various social situations.

* It is possible to identify developmental levels in the perception of complexity within friendship, related to general cognitive development, as late as the stage of late adolescence. Selman (1980) demonstrated stages of hierarchical development compatible with the structural conceptions characteristic of Piaget and Kohlberg. However, as La Gaipa notes (1981) we have no adequate explanation for the fact that certain children move on from one given conceptual level to a higher one while others do not. Again, in friendship as in other social spheres, moving on to a higher level of thinking is not guaranteed by chronological development (Flavell, 1977)

* It is important to note that, in contrast to the development theories which we have cited, there is evidence which contradicts the assumption of a developmental hierarchy. Research in social learning discuss the accumulation of knowledge in functional learning and do not subscribe to the idea of a chronological cognitive hierarchy (Maccoby, 1968; Bandura, 1969; Brody, 1977).

Furthermore, since descriptions of developmental stages were based on interviews with or compositions by children, they may represent progress in social IQ which may not necessarily be reflected in a friendship interaction. **An individual may possess the basic intellectual and communicative capacity for friendship and not be able to put it into practice.** Introverted or high IQ children often exhibit such characteristics.

* La Gaipa and counselors and educators ask: why is it important to know where the child or adolescent may be in terms of developmental perceptions of friendship? It would seem that children whose developmental expectations are below the average for their age-group, will have a higher chance of being socially rejected.
* The evidence, both that cited above and other, points to two basic qualities that adolescents value highly in friendship: loyalty and intimacy. These two qualities reflect the factors characterizing the transition from childhood to adulthood.

Chapter Three: The Singular Import of Friendship During the Adolescent Period

The adolescent period is characterized by physical, emotional and social changes; at the same time societal demands put maturational pressures on the child. Friendship and support plays a vital role in the adolescent's ability to cope with the changes and demands.

The transition from childhood to adulthood places the following tasks before the developing child:
 * separating from parents
 * forming a personal identity
 * integrating with the social system

Interaction with and support from peers enables the adolescent to perform these tasks successfully. In addition, he will need the continued help of his family. In fact, the adolescent may seek and find support from three sources or circles of association:

Age Cohort or (Distant) Peer Group. The widest circle is that of the age cohort or peer group. These are others in a similar stage of development: the transition from childhood to adulthood and maturity. The individual adolescent finds a mirror of himself and an identification model in his age cohort. The group serves as trailblazer, norm-setter, status giver. Members are to be found in all areas of social functioning around the world. The adolescent sees them, hears about them, basks in their glory, is identified with them and learns from them. The age cohort can serve the individual adolescent as a stage for an unlimited repertoire of response, alternatives of expectation, judgment, identification and role playing, thus aiding him in forming his identity and fashioning his life-style.

(Close) Peer Groups. The second circle consists of the various groups to which the adolescent belongs to in various stages of various periods of his extended adolescence, an overall period of 10-15 years.

These groups include formal and informal affiliation, located in the neighborhood, at school or church, in the scouts or other youth movements, in community center settings, in camp, in the army, at work. Each of these contexts provides: a forum to belong to, an arena of experience in active role-playing, and a reserve of potential friends; who will be needed at a certain stage in the adolescent's development as factors in a support-system for the advancement of his separation from his parents and for the fashioning of an experimental identi-kit, which will gradually develop into his personal identity.

Circle of Friends. The third circle consists of the friends, both intimate and less close, that one has during the adolescent period. These friends have been chosen from the wider group of friends held in reserve to support him in his development, or who have chosen him to support them in theirs. Since friends change according to needs, it is important to see the role played by peer groups in the development of adolescents and note the function of different types of friends.

1. The Importance of Peer Groups[2]

The term "peer groups" includes formal groups (classes in school, youth groups) as well as informal groups (cliques from a formal group, neighborhood groups). It is not our purpose here to discuss the differences between the various kinds of peer groups, but rather the function of the peer groups in the life of the adolescent and the manner in which this function is fulfilled. We shall discuss the unique role of friends, both intimate and not, at certain stages of the developmental process, within the seven major functions of peer groups in the adolescent process.

Peer groups fulfill seven major functions in the adolescent process:

---

[2] Sociologists, psychologists and educators use various terms, which are often synonymous, such as age cohort, peer group, etc. For the purposes of this discussion, and in order to prevent misunderstandings, we propose the following definitions, our guiding criteria being mainly the size of population, depth of bond, and function of relationship:

Age Cohort-all adolescents, or any particular group of them, without personal bonds or commitments between them, although they share

Support

Adolescents undergo new internal and external experiences. They cannot get necessary support from their parents because they are adults and at a different experiential stage of life, and because adolescence itself entails the need to separate from parents and its attendant difficulties in the adolescent-parent relationship. Members of peer groups within the age cohort have the same problems, are undergoing the same types of changes, physical and emotional, and are capable to supplying mutual support through sharing their personal, internal experiences (i.e., the awakening of sexual desire, doubts about values and behavior patterns accepted by the family, society, and "establishment", dreams of the future).

Peer support is vital for the adolescent who is experiencing ups and downs of his self image, whether his developmental pattern conforms to the "storm and stress" definition of psychoanalysis or whether it is more gradual and continuous.

---

criteria of similarity and common needs and may participate in common activities.

Peers-People one knows and has chosen as a group of reference and common transaction, in the neighborhood, community, youth group, classroom, etc.

Friends-A group that is defined and stable at a given time; it may be limited to 4-5 members (clique), or, in certain cases, larger (6-12 members). The members of the group share a social and emotional relationship, a certain degree of self-disclosure and mutual support. They engage in regular common activities, such as hanging out together, going to the beach or to the movies, visiting with each other at home, etc.

Intimate Friends-A small number (1-4) of friends who, at a given time, attain a profound degree of mutual self-revelation, emotional dependence and unconditional mutual support.

Positive Peer Support Group-A stable group organized as a forum for common learning and positive mutual support for the purpose of self-development, shaping of personal identity and development of the ability to cope. In this volume this term will be used to denote the peer support group organized in accordance with our approach or for parallel purposes. It is referred to from now on as a PPS group.

Social Comparison

The peer group not only serves as a source of support, but also provides a forum for systematic and active social role playing (boy/girl, leader/follower, good student/bad student) which enables him to compare himself to others within his age cohort. The need for such social comparison is particularly strong because the adolescent is in the process of formulating his identity. He evaluates himself relative to others in his age cohort. The cohort sets the norms and determines the criteria of acceptable behavior, modes of dress, modes of thought, and opinions on various subjects. The adolescent measures himself against these norms, both consciously and subconsciously, and draws on these criteria in guiding himself towards his identity. Thus, with his burgeoning biological change and awakening sexual desire, he may compare the development of his sexual organs, his sexual fantasies and behavior in order to verify that he is sexually normal. Peer groups offer the adolescent a variety of frames of reference, supplying different models and varying norms in addition to or instead of those supplied by the adult world of family and society.

Models to Imitate and Pressure to Experiment

Not only does the adolescent find a variety of alternative behaviors, but he also finds certain people who actively initiate experiences of a certain nature. Those peers who have reached a stage where they are capable of doing certain things (like maintain a relationship with someone of the opposite sex, face a conflict with another adolescent or an adult) help those who have not reached that stage either directly by serving as an example, carrying them along with him in such an activity, or by pressuring them to do it "too", or indirectly by serving as a model to imitate. Sharing experiences of various participants in the peer group provides the adolescent indirect or vicarious achievement through experiencing events through fantasy and emotion, as if he himself was actively participating. Our interviews with adolescents in Israel and the United States revealed that the reports of adolescents of things that "we did" did not necessarily mean he personally did them. It did mean that he was part of a group which discussed, planned or shared such an experience. This discovery is particularly important for group leaders who have had experiences where they thought they had caught adolescents lying and have tried to "reform" their behavior.

Mirror and Compass

The marginal position during the transition between childhood and adulthood means that adolescents lack a stable and well-defined sense of self. The patterns formed during childhood are losing their validity and the realm of possible and desired vis a vis feelings, decisions and actions is blurred and uncertain. The peer group serves the adolescent as a mirror of himself. They serve to reflect back a picture of himself-a thermometer, barometer and compass to be used in evaluating his own development-actual and desired. A large part of an adolescent's self-esteem is a function of the reaction of others to him and their opinion of him. The exchange of experiences among peer group members, and their discussion of the significance of things, supports the adolescent's cognitive development and affective readiness to think similarly-when he is by himself, with a friend or with a group of friends.

Status, Power and Authority

Belonging to a peer group also serves as a source of a sense of power, status and authority, or, as Benton (1975) calls it, a sense of "ourselves against the world."

The adolescent's rapid biological and cognitive development gives rise to great expectations, but his status-legal, economic and organizational-in relation to his family, personnel in the school or the work place, or other adults, is still inferior. Peer groups provide status symbols, such as special jargon, special styles of dress and make-up, special music, etc. as well as a social climate and support. In other words, as in any selective club of a social elite, the peer group allows the adolescent a feeling of membership in a social, status-giving group, which makes him feel unique. The adolescent needs this feeling in his struggle against the frames of reference and norms of the older generation, which has power and authority over him. He needs it, as well, because he is experiencing the loneliness and lack of confidence typical of those who are in a period of transition and in a marginal position: the adolescent is no longer a child, but has not yet gained confirmation of his majority.

Support in Differentiation from Parents
The peer group serves a special purpose in the adolescent's process of differentiation from his parents. Up until this point parents and family have provided the main frame of reference and authority for the adolescent. As adolescents challenge the norms of social behavior and expectations set by their parents, the peer group offers a selection of alternates and strengthens the assumption that in a changing world the new generation has a right to self-realization in accordance with its own conceptions, feelings and plans. In addition, since some of these feelings are related to the intensification of erotic and aggressive impulses directed against the parents, as described by psychoanalysis, the peer group provides a neutral zone where the adolescent can relax and even ventilate such feelings. Most of the time the adolescent does not lose the support of his family, but gains an additional source of support which complements and balances the power, authority and variety of norms during the period of his struggle to differentiate from his parents and shape a personal identity.

A Prototype for Future Social Relations
Peer group transactions serve as prototypes of relationship behavior in later life: social patterns of relationships, work patterns, patterns of relationships with members of the opposite sex, and political patterns of behavior. Peer group transactions provide opportunities to learn different ways of interacting, examining social behavior, developing interests and skills which are significant at a given time, sharing in the presentation and discussion of problems, expressing feelings-all of which and more are necessary for the adolescent.

2. How A Peer Group Functions and Exerts Influence
In view of the many functions of the peer group, it is particularly important to understand exactly how the processes of influence work within the peer group. Several factors operate within the group and shape the mode of activity as well as the power for influence.
* The structure of the surroundings and the actual site of common activities help determine the relationships within the group. Thus, the shape of the room and the seating arrangement greatly affects relationships which will form within the group. Sometimes the

physical position of the members of the group within the room itself constitutes a criterion for the nature of the subsequent relationships and the internal group hierarchy (who sits next to whom, the distance between one child and another, who is alone and who is sitting together, etc.).

* The social context in which the activity is taking place. Thus, behavior in a classroom will be less formal than behavior in a new or unfamiliar place; behavior at a sporting event will be more competitive and aggressive than at a party, etc.
* The clarity of one's role definition. If the individual perceives his role and the stimulation to play his role in a vague manner, he will rely more on the opinions of the others. Similarly, if expectations are clear and what he is to do is detailed, the individual will adjust better.
* Feedback from the group to the individual will largely determine his attitude towards the group and his satisfaction in terms of being part of it. Thus, if his actions and opinions stimulate positive reinforcement, he will think more highly of the members of the group.
* Size and stability of the group itself will determine the decision-making process. Thus a small and cohesive group will agree more quickly on various subjects than a larger more diffuse group.
* Certain personality traits, such as dependency or anxiety, may intensify the influence potential of the peer group. The child's status within the group will also determine the degree to which it may influence his behavior. Those children holding low status in a group will submit more readily to pressure from a leader or peer group than those children having higher status. Devotion to the norms of the peer group arises from the adolescent's status within the group and his desire to gain higher status. Feeling of belonging and approval are central factors in any friendship.

It is important to note at this point that these various factors form an integrated whole, and no single factor may be considered as solely responsible for peer group influence.

The importance of the peer group varies according to different cultures and socioeconomic background although the processes we have described are common to all peer groups. In western, heterogeneous urban society, characterized by bewildering change, the peer group plays a very important role in socializing the individual. It may even take the place of parents in terms of enforcing and interpreting a moral code.

Ideology and general belief system of a culture and which are expressed in education also influences the structure and function of a PPS group. Thus, societies which value cooperation and collectivism as a social aim (such as on the kibbutz) will place greater emphasis on peer groups than societies which value the individual as an agent of social change. Socioeconomic background also makes a difference: middle class parents emphasize independence and internalized standards of behavior which results in their children conforming less to their peer groups' standards; however, children of lower socioeconomic backgrounds reflect more dependence on their peer group as they conform more closely to peer group standards.

3. Peer Group Activity: How It Serves the Individual

Despite the overall implications mentioned above, the different constituents of different groups means that the significance of membership may vary from group to group. Thus, membership in an informal neighborhood peer group is not comparable to membership in a football team or a scout troop or a particular school class. Each group is structured around its own aims and purposes, its own organizational framework, its own leadership requirements, etc. Such self-defined aims constitutes a defined ecological system for patterns of social interaction.

Although structured groups have their own defined aims and patterns of interaction and are instrumental in providing for the anticipated and defined needs of their creator/members, each individual within the group fashions what Kurt Lewin calls his own "life space" within the group context. He develops patterns of transaction and friendship which are uniquely his own and which spring from the basic components of his personality and particular needs at any given time.

Group membership serves the individual in four principal ways, whether it is a pair-friendship, a group of three, or a larger, structured group.

1. It provides a **stage** on which one may present himself according to alternative images and patterns of behavior.
2. It serves as a **mirror** providing feedback by reflecting how significant others view one's behavior.
3. It gives access to demonstration of **models** of alternatives in values and behavior patterns in different situations.
4. It provides systematic and defined behavior **training**, such as in a sports team, an art class, a school lesson; or a micro-community system such as a neighborhood peer group. Within these groups the individual repeats certain behavior patterns in different ways, creating stimuli and responses which further his personal social development.

What the above systems have in common in contributing to the development of the individual may be defined in a different way by means of Festinger's theory of social comparison (Festinger, 1954), which characterizes the process of learning and development by repeated comparison with significant others and by means of his theory of cognitive dissonance. Cognitive dissonance represents the disharmony which occurs when an individual comes into a group with certain values, attitudes and behavior patterns and encounters alternative possibilities of perceiving a situation and alternative responses to these perceptions. Such disharmony produces a powerful stimulus and sometimes a normative crisis. It calls into question patterns of conceptualizing and behavior, undermining the internal equilibrium established over the long, childhood, socialization period. The loss of this internal equilibrium pushes the individual to search for alternatives and thus to advance to the next stage of development. In terms of our approach to encouraging the individual's psycho-social development by means of PPS groups, this reaction to the disturbance of inner equilibrium is vital.

4. The Significance of Friends During Adolescence

Friends also fill many of the needs which are fulfilled by peer groups. Their contribution comes about through involvement and commitment growing deeper as the friendship bond develops. Friendship can be said to fulfill five principal functions. **Providing Additional Components to the One's Identity**

The problematic nature of modern society which on the surface offers unlimited choice, seems to make it very difficult for the adolescent to be somebody. Society is extremely complex and involuted and undergoing rapid change with an uncertain and vague future. Sex role patterns, social behavioral norms and community institutions have lost their firm definition. There are family crises and other problems arising from the lack of constancy. The process of fashioning an identity, which occurs over a long period of time-10-15 years-is extremely complex and requires a high level of coping ability in the sense of both social cognition and social skills. The adolescent must determine who he is, who he wishes to be, and who he can be-based on his basic personality traits, his past, the ecological system within which he functions and his dreams for the future. Our interviews with adolescents show that in order to put together this composite sketch from conditions and experiences which are meaningful in the present and promising for the future, the adolescent must gather various components of personal identity and sexual role and fashion them into a certain entity. Since the adolescent does not know what he wants to be, taking into consideration what he is capable of being, he must draw various components of personal identity and sexual role out of the reserves significant for his age cohort, particularly among those in the various peer groups of which he is a member. As has been noted above, the adolescent chooses friends according to the needs of the moment which he feels possess components significant for him. He makes friends with these individuals, experiences the significance of certain qualities which they possess, and borrows those which seem suitable for himself. He then examines the qualities which he has acquired and attempts to adapt them to himself. At the point at which the friend has no more to offer, he may use various means of rejection in order to get rid of him.

Intimacy in Freely Expressing Emotions

A heterogeneous and more impersonal peer group cannot provide a forum for intimacy which can be attained between one or two friends. A candidate for an "intimate friend" is chosen at a given time, for a given period of time, who is compatible both cognitively and affectively with certain needs, some of which have been described above and others of which will be described below. In the company of such a friend, the adolescent feels freer to express repressed feelings of anger and anxiety, motives for rebellion, perceptions of situations, plans of response, etc. without fearing criticism or lack of empathy which might occur in the larger peer group. The closeness of friends such as these, their free behavior toward each other and their sense of empathy with each other, means that they may criticize each other and learn to borrow and change behavior and ideational patterns without fear of being misunderstood or rejected.

Understanding and Acceptance

Interviews with adolescents and sessions of PPS groups have repeatedly revealed the expectation that "my friend will understand me and accept me as I am." This kind of unconditional acceptance is difficult and even impossible within a larger peer group. In addition to the need for support, discussed in the section about PPS groups, even in matters where their deeds and opinions might not be popular, there is a need for intimacy with friends-the possibility to be completely open and frank with someone who is equally open and frank with them. Adults, too, seek understanding and acceptance from their friends. The difference is that in adolescence the friends involved are egocentric-they both still feel they are the center of the world; that their problems, ideas, suggestions, are unique; that all eyes are upon them; that they need understanding and acceptance in order to formulate another aspect of their personality out of various components; and that others must understand and accept them. Friendship in adolescence develops out of an emotional-and at the same time pragmatic and functional-approach of two individuals, each one of whom is immersed in himself and too preoccupied with himself to make much of an investment in the other person, although he may often feel and claim that he is very interested in him. At some points in the friendship the adolescent friend may behave like a rational philosopher; at other times he may become target-centered and practical; then, again, he may be sensitive and anxious about any reaction. It may be expected that this egocentricity will arouse a hostile and aggressive reaction, as it often does in parents, teachers and peers. Friends, however, are dependent upon each other and may be, therefore, more willing to provide the understanding, acceptance and support which their friend need; at any rate, they are willing to do this at certain times and within certain limits, in order to maintain the friendship. They often accept the situation out of fear of being abandoned by the friend who picked them out of the reserve of potential friends and relieved their fears of unending loneliness while he was, in effect, seeking to fulfill his own needs.

Fulfillment of Mutual Needs

Adolescent friendships develop despite the endemic ego-centricity, because friends provide and complement each other with the traits, interests and behavior patterns which each lacks. An adolescent has many needs which he has difficulty in fulfilling, because he is going through a period of internal as well as external changes-changes in feelings, relationships, and behavior, at home, at school, etc. and changes in his expectations and plans for the future. When he finds a friend, or when someone chooses him as a friend, they are mutually indispensable because each will give the other what he has and take from him what he needs. Because he has many needs and because these needs change, the adolescent needs a variety of friends. He needs to be able to regulate the degree of intimacy with any given friend and to change friends in a certain rotation, the peer group serving as a sort of holding tank of potential friends from whom he makes his choices.

Establishing Long-Term Relationships

Just as the peer group serves as the prototype for social relations later in life, so do adolescent friendships serve as the prototype for future social relationships. The transactions involved in the close relationships of adolescent experience shape the nature of his future relationships, his individual and family needs, his professional or business career, the nature of his political activity, etc. Development of cognitive capacity, urging of parents and teachers, and the influence of mass media enable the adolescent to face the future. Certain friendships are significant not only in terms of fulfilling his immediate needs, but also in terms of indicating his future life style. Despite the adolescent's cognitive capacity, he is often unaware of this connection with the future. It is therefore important that the effect of present friendships in terms of future needs be pointed out to him. Such an awareness will aid him in understanding how some friends will be temporary and others will become long-term associates. Even more importantly, by helping the adolescent understand the temporary nature of certain friendship, such an awareness will enable him to cope when the friendship ends.

5. Expectations of Friends

The following questions were asked in personal interviews and sessions of PPS groups:

"What do you look for in a friend?"

"What is the significance of the friendship process?"

"When does a friend stop being important?"

The answers formed a **matrix** consisting of three **horizontal** and three **vertical** dimensions.

Three **focal** points of support emerged:

* Support in processing feelings and concepts and in dealing with them on an internal level.
* Support in confronting significant others (parents, teachers, peers)
* Support in confronting unfamiliar elements

Three **patterns** of support emerged:

* Listening and empathy
* Active support
* Teaching and instructing

The following statements by adolescents illustrate the three patterns of support.

On Listening and Empathy

"I can tell my girl friend whatever I'm feeling at the moment without thinking twice, and I know that she'll listen to me; she cares about me more than about others; she is with me even when she disagrees with me; I can depend on her to understand me and feel with me; she is like me though we are very different; I tell her everything and I know that she will keep my secrets; she's like Dear Abbey for me; without her I'm lonely."

On Active Participation

"I tell her things and she tells me frankly what she thinks is right and what isn't; she knows what she wants and gives me the strength to want things too; she helps me with my homework whenever I need help and she won't let me fail; he will fight for me even against someone stronger than himself; I argue with her, but actually I'm arguing with myself; he helps me in arguments with my parents; I can argue or even fight with him; the two of us together are the controlling power in the neighborhood; she will fight for me; I feel secure in any situation with her."

On Teaching and Instructing

"I learn how to behave from her; she does what I don't dare to do; he is an example for me; he is what I would like to be; I imitate him just like a monkey does, though that is not a nice way of saying it."

In most cases adolescents expect intimacy and support in everything; that is, they expect their friend to listen to them, support them and instruct them-both in their internal struggles and in their confrontations with others. What is common to most adolescents is their egocentric orientation-I am the focal point and the question is what the friendship does **for me**, what the friend means **to me**. Gradually there is a shift towards mutuality-I help my friend, I give to him, I listen to him.

The function of friendship can be seen as developing towards a service-orientation, dynamic, differentiated according to personal needs. It is possible to see these needs in the statements quoted below. Adolescents, going through a process by which various elements of their self image, their opinions, their conceptualizations, their attitudes and their function in the world are being questioned, see themselves as needing:

A. Someone to Listen to Them. This expectation appears in every version of the answers to the question "What do you expect of a good friend?"

B. Someone to Bolster Their Confidence. To supply those deficiencies which shake their self-confidence. Someone who "will be with me when I'm lonely; will allow me to compare my opinions with his, so that I can see other ways of doing things; will tell me when I'm right, so that I will really be sure that I'm doing the right thing; will help me with my homework; will lend me money; will show understanding when I'm punished at home; will help me when I'm in a fight or about to be beaten up; will walk me home at night; will take my side when I confront my parents."

C. Someone to Help Them Learn and Develop a Social IQ. Someone who will bare his feelings and be willing to reveal what he does in certain situations-when confronting a parent, for example, or in relations with a member of the opposite sex, or when confronted with social pressures, etc. This last function seems extremely important, in view of the emphasis placed on it in our interviews with both adolescents and adults. Women, for instance, report how they learned to deal with their husbands or adolescent sons from friends; others reported how they learned to deal with their boss, etc. Beyond the individual stories we see a developing process of verification for the purpose of examining one's ability to cope with expectations, pressures, and the need to respond within one's interpersonal functioning in various social contexts. This is also true for adolescents, however, for them learning from a friend has a particular significance. The need for a friend is central and fundamental. He is in a marginal position, between childhood and adulthood, and he needs figures who can challenge him with notional and substantive alternatives. Such figures can be found in the various peer groups available to him: class, school, youth group, neighborhood, etc. **He chooses friends out of the pool of possibilities who either seem to be like him or fill in with qualities which he is lacking**. The adolescent wishes to be like one of his friends, to acquire the information he controls, to learn the skill he has and assumes that he will gradually fill in his lacks through his friends. In individual interviews and group sessions adolescent peers show awareness of the fact that a friend has needs of his own and is not just someone who is willing to and who should serve them. In certain aspects, however, that is what they expect of their friends although they are prepared for a certain degree of reciprocity in return.

When the adolescent is in need of a different model, he will weaken his relationship with an existing friend and try to choose another candidate out of the reserve of potential friends within the peer groups of which he is a member or trying to join. There is, of course, great variation in the active initiation of acquiring friends and shaping friendships. Some plan and execute an active campaign; others wait and respond to the attraction or initiatory activities of others.

Thus, **a friend can be defined as one who complements and supports one in the process of differentiation and integration in each of the dimensions mentioned above, and helps the development of both social cognition and social skills.** The ability to find a friend, develop a friendship and then to terminate the friendship represents the ability to ensure oneself sources of complementing necessary for reorientation and personal integration in a certain direction and on a certain level of functioning. The friend or friends-whether parallel or consecutive-constitute the nucleus of the fundamental support system of peers. Peer groups, which we have discussed, serve the adolescent as the source of either active players on the "teams" of which he is a member or "on the bench players" from among whom active players may be chosen to fill vacated places.

Another way of representing the significance of friendship in adolescence is to picture the adolescent as an actor playing in a creative dramatics role enacted on a series of interlocking, circular stages. The adolescent develops his part from an open-ended play consisting of a simple outline written by an invisible playwright, the social system.

In order to understand and define himself, according to what is expected of him in a developing transaction in various cycles of function, the adolescent chooses a friend from among the peers in his ecological system-either on his own initiative or in response to the initiative of others with similar needs. He draws closer to the friend/ and expects the friend to draw closer to him. With the support of his friend he attempts to achieve authentication in a certain sphere. Sometimes he has several friends, each one fulfilling his needs in a different cycle or function. Since there is a difference between his qualities and needs and those of each one of his potential friends, there is a different distance and a different pattern of transaction between him and each one of his friends. In the process of his development he needs their complementation and support, as they need his in their parallel process of development.

Having examined the significance of friends and friendship for the adolescent, we will attempt to describe the process through which friendship develops, including the various stages in the relationship.

Chapter Four: The Development of Friendship During Adolescence

1. Shaping Identity through Peers and Friends

Certain patterns in conceptualizations of the meaning of friendship showed up in response to questions asked of adolescents in individual interviews or in the course of sessions of PPS groups, such as "Why did you choose that particular friend?", "What does this friendship give you?", "How are you and your friend alike?" and "How has the friendship changed you? How has it changed your friend?" The process clearly is cognitive (sometimes unconscious) with an affective basis. The adolescent approaches a particular individual, whether consciously or not, out of a sense or assumption that this individual possess certain elements which will fit into the mosaic of his personal identity and coping ability. Or, conversely, he is attracted to another as a means of serving the other's similar needs. Sometimes the work of "completing the mosaic" is real and very practical and sometimes it is ideal and notional-searching for someone who is part of one's dream of shaping a personal identity and sensing that a certain element has been found in the complex personality of the one chosen to be friend. Examples of answers to our questions follow:

* "He was the way I wanted to appear."
* "She shows me how it should be done."
* "She understood why I act the way I do."
* "She listened to me. I poured out everything I felt, and when I saw how she listened to me, I understood that I didn't have the patience to listen like that, although it is very important to me to have someone listen to me."
* "He helped me to say no-first to myself and then to others. I'm the kind of person who doesn't dare insist; others have the courage to do that."

* "She is able to look inside-deep into herself and into others. I'm the kind of person who runs away from looking inside...She uncovered what I didn't dare uncover."
* "I find it easier to deny things that happen to me or that I feel, instead of facing them. He is the kind of person I would like to be but can't."

These and other statements can be divided into categories of elements complementing basic personality traits or expectations for shaping identity and behavior patterns. At every stage of adolescence friends are chosen from the pool of potential people in the peer group who are at the same level of development. He chooses those individuals who can be instrumental in complementing his cognitive system which the transition from childhood to adulthood has undermined and which is being formed and shaped towards maturity. By means of the chosen friend the adolescent restores various parts of the complex mosaic of his existing identity, adds new elements which seem missing and desirable, examines-by means of reflection-the significance of this complementation, and borrows, from this friend or another, a partial or complete model for identification and emulation. Some of these borrowed elements are then displayed for purposes of examination and reaction to the friend or peer group. Sometimes this process takes the form of outward negation of an element, despite its use. Sometimes, after repeated examination, the element is accepted or rejected. Acceptance means integrating this artificial transplant into existing elements. Rejecting the transplant is followed by a renewed search for other elements.

The following questions were posed: In which of the following categories (cognitive, emotional, social) are you like/unlike your friend? What do you think you got from your friend? What do you think you gave to your friend? In mapping the answers, we discovered a very complex pattern of dynamics of need fulfillment. The adolescents felt that their friends fulfilled their needs; according to our further interpretation, friends are instrumental in helping to fashion the adolescent's identity and in helping him deal with problems.

Some answers are seemingly simple: "I was looking for someone who would listen to me." "I wanted someone to understand me." "I expected someone to help me." etc. However, many of the answers to clarification questions such as "help with what?" "understand what?" or "what kind of feedback?" contain a description of processes of filling gaps in the vague system of shaping a personal identity. Although the confrontation may be with teachers, parents or peers, in a deeper sense all these are but an intermediary variable in the internal struggle for self-clarification and personal reorientation. In certain cases there is ambivalence in feeling or in the sense of the needs of the self at a given time. As one adolescent girl put it, "I don't dare be aggressive; I'd like to be active, but I'm not really prepared to be, and I need a friend to do it for me-to animate me, to raise me to a higher level and a quicker pace of functioning."

An analysis of PPS group sessions and individual interviews indicates that adolescents seek to fulfill their needs through their friends at varying stages of development within their ecological system. Every adolescent has certain assumptions, based on his conceptualizations and feelings vis a vis which social role he would like to play. He plays out certain roles in his interpersonal interactions guided by these assumptions and he seeks out friends who would make it possible for him to play the role he has chosen. Of course, a considerable part of this ongoing jigsaw puzzle-like "drama" is neither conscious nor "real," since most adolescents do not yet understand their "life script," what they fear, what part of a complementary pair is theirs or the process of their own and their friend's personal development.

2. Stages of Friendship
A. Entering into and Shaping a Friendship

The first stage of friendship consists of developing a readiness for friendship with a particular individual or individuals. Three main problems can appear at this point and must be worked through before one can continue on to the next stage.

* There is a tendency to limit oneself to a friendship with a single person who is expected to satisfy a multitude of needs. It is a rare individual who can meet such a variety of needs; furthermore, a termination of this friendship leaves a vacuum and a deep wound.

Therefore, adolescents should become aware that it is possible and even desirable to develop various friendships in different areas; it is possible to teach adolescents through alternative experiences that it is possible to develop friendship with one person to do homework, another to play a game in which both are interested, another with whom to engage in political activity, still another to do community volunteer work with, and yet another with whom to attend cultural or entertainment activities. The greater the number of alternatives, the deeper the understanding of the nature of interpersonal interaction, the richer the physical, cognitive and affective development and the more certain the adolescent will develop a multi-directional life-scope. It is possible to help the adolescent to understand that the depth of involvement and mutual commitment should not, and can not, be the same with every friend. Indeed, mutual acquaintance and activity should be allowed to lead gradually to define the significance of the friendship with each person involved. Thus, a deep, mutual commitment and involvement will develop with one or several of his various friends.

* A lack of awareness of the essential nature of his relationship with his friend or friends and the nature of his own needs and expectations.

He should learn to ask himself questions about what led him (or the friends) into the relationship; who his friends are (in the sense of what sort of people they are) and what sort of influence they have on his development in certain defined areas (like whether they influence who his other friends are, how he spends his leisure time, what his ultimate values and behavior patterns are, etc.). He needs to be aware how different friendships fulfill different needs. Sometimes the activity is formally defined: developing a certain skill, using leisure time well, fulfilling social functions, competing for social status, etc. At other times aims are not defined. The aims of friendship often determine the nature of joint activities and possible rewards.

There are various ways of developing the awareness required for coping with social situations; it is important to make sure that each participant in the group has opportunities to make social comparisons and examine the significance of friendship within the context of developing his self-image and personal identity. He should be able to ask himself what he is gaining from the friendship in terms of developing his identity, experience in dealing with different situations and if he is reaching a higher level of functioning. He needs to ask himself: with whom he is competing, what he wants to prove, how this will affect his confidence and readiness to enter into further experiences, and what price he is paying in other areas of his life and/or within his relationships with other people. He needs to ask himself how this friendship is related to his dreams of shaping his identity and constructing a life-style.

* The issue of acceptance and rejection, both by people whose friendship is being sought and by groups or cliques of adolescents of which he wishes to become a member.

A distinction must be made between formal and informal groups. A formal group, such as a sports team, consists of a certain number of members and makes specific decisions through specific people or persons accepting or rejecting bids for membership. Those who are rejected are clearly not members of the group. An informal group-in the neighborhood, in school or in a youth group-has less clearly drawn lines and a person may remain on the fringe of the group and gradually establish oneself as part of the group, adapting to the group expectations and becoming friendly with more established members. In this manner, by means of different strategies the individual may gradually gain power and authority and claim a certain status.

When a person attempts to gain admittance to an existing group of friends, he is uncertain about his chances of success. He may develop anxieties, faulty cognitive judgment, ambivalent feelings and behavior. It is important for the individual to be able to distinguish between the attempt to grasp the factors of the situation into which one wishes to be accepted and the development of social skills necessary in order to enter into the situation. PPS groups facilitate development in these two aspects as well as serve the adolescent in an additional respect: providing him with a supportive social framework during this period of transition. The very fact of belonging to a peer group guided by an adult leader assures him of not being isolated and of having repeated possibilities of experiencing a variety of situations.

B. Maintaining Continuity in Friendship

The second stage of development is learning how to maintain a friendship established with a significant other. This is the problem of maintaining continuity within the relationship. Some individuals make a tremendous effort to be accepted by others and are willing to pay any price in order not to lose the friendship once established. Allen (1981) invokes the dissonance theory (Festinger, 1957) indicating that the greater the effort made to enter a group, the greater the value of acceptance into it; the greater the value of the acceptance, the greater the price he is willing to pay for it and the higher his esteem for the group. Thus, an unpopular child who has succeeded in making a friend or being accepted into a peer group will set a high value on this acceptance and will be willing to pay a greater price in order to continue the friendship than would a child who was accepted easily. Experiences in a PPS group are meant to provide opportunities to attain skill in maintaining a relationship for as long as desired and to examine the nature of the satisfaction gained from the various friendships as well as the personal cost paid for each relationship. Particularly, adolescents need to develop skills in maintaining the balance of reinforcement necessary to ensure continuity within a significant friendship for as long as desired and in self-examination as well as in observing his surroundings in order to be able to evaluate the demands being made on him and the role he is to take within the relationship, both interpersonal and within the group.

C. Breaking Up A Friendship

How can an adolescent escape from a friendship relationship which he no longer wants with a minimum of damage, both to him and to others? This, thus, is the third stage of the friendship process: its end. Just as awareness and skills developed by appropriate experiences are necessary in the previous stages of the friendship process, they are also necessary now. A friendship has been formed and maintained in order to fulfill certain needs of the individual or group. However, once there is no more need for the friendship, it can continue out of inertia or an unwillingness to deal with the fact that the friendship is no longer desirable. Group experiences developed specifically for the purpose can teach how to create a sequence of transactions in which the involvement is gradually lessened until the individual can extricate himself from the emotional and organizational bonds. Such experiential learning can even indicate when it might be appropriate to end a relationship abruptly, using as non-destructive approach as is possible. Indeed, it is possible to view this third stage as extremely important in the psycho-social continuum of development.

* It is important to end a friendship when it is no longer meaningful or desired. A crisis of this type may be potentially positive in terms of the individual's development if he knows how to deal with it.
* Given practice in dealing with a large number of possible crisis situations can help the individual emerge from the crisis with a minimum of distress. A break-up with a friend tends to cause a great deal of distress especially occurring as it does at the stage of development when an adolescent is facing a disintegration of his biological equilibrium and his values system. Many adolescents exhibit the maturational pattern of "storm and stress" and are particularly vulnerable and sensitive. Thus the PPS group can provide guided experience of many potential crisis situations, prevent the usual distress and provide therapeutic support. Evidence from the adolescents themselves as well as from various studies indicates that the rapid rate of turnover in friendships is a normative occurrence. Therefore, they need to be able to realize it is not evidence of personal failure and a reason to withdraw.
* Many adolescents feel that everyone is aware of their failure and is standing in judgment. This is a result of adolescent egocentricity and it is important to help the individual understand that the reality may be quite different. What really matters is how they feel about the place of a given friendship in their lives; this subject is central to them and the other side of the friendship, but not central to anyone else.
* Severe, negative reactions to a breakup of a friendship can be mitigated by support from an alternative friendship and from adults who are aware of the situation. Appropriate group experiences can show how parallel friendships can be developed not only as a means of enriching the individual's social development, but also as a means of preventing such severe crisis. Thus, friendships can be broken off gradually while simultaneously developing alternative possibilities of satisfying needs.

3. The Need for a Variety of Potential Friends

During the long and complicated period of development, the child requires a variety of friends to provide him support as he copes with the tasks related to growing up: shaping his identity, forming his value system, learning how to cope. Such a variety of potential friends, from which he feels he has a right to choose those who will meet his needs at any given time, can come from a systematic establishment of a reserve in the form of group of peers from each circle in which he functions. The following descriptions indicate the extent of the variety:

* "J. is my closest friend. We stay up half the night talking; he is the kind of person I'd like to be. With R. I do my homework and his mother cooks and feeds us-not like my mother who is always busy working. S. is just a friend who sometimes joins us when there is nothing to do and we talk about this and that; sometimes we talk about girls and sex and other junk. He is the one who gets into fights and mouths off to the teachers. I'll never be like that, but he is a friend."

* "D. and Y. are my friends in the youth group. The three of us are leaders for the younger groups. I don't want to be like them, and I can't. But together we get the job done. No, we are not alike. D. is a sensitive type and I can't be like him. No I don't know if I want to be like him. The girls like him a lot. Y. is like a bulldozer-he can get things done in no time."

* "In the neighborhood I don't have a 'real' friend. But there is a kind of a gang, with Y. and R. and others, and we sometimes hang out together. To tell the truth, Y. sometimes does things that I'm dying to do, but don't dare. I get into fights with R, but not seriously. He's taking up Judo. I'm not like that, but...he means something to me."

The interviews point clearly to the pattern of adolescents forming friendships with a variety of people, each one meeting different needs and gradually being collected from a pool of potential friends found in the individual's various circles of peers. It may be surmised that there is also a gradual turnover in friends as friendships are broken off at the point they have ceased being functional and other friendships are formed to take their place. The friend who is no longer functional is either dropped altogether or simply loses his status as a close, active friend.

Within this structure it is clear that a variety of friendships meets a

vital and fundamental need in adolescence. Therefore, those who do not know how to make friends or how to maintain a friendship once formed have a problem. The PPS group we are proposing has three objectives which should answer this problem:
* Provide a pool of potential friends and peers.
* Provide systematic experiences aimed at enlarging perceptions of friendship and improving the social skill needed in order to develop friendship.
* Provide a supportive forum aimed at enabling mutual support, feedback and alternatives appropriate to various developmental needs.

4. Difficulties and Conflicts in Friendship

The need to be part of a peer group or to be someone's friend is extremely powerful. Most adolescents succeed in becoming integrated into a peer group and in making friends. The process is, however, accompanied by difficulties and conflicts, some of which will be discussed below.

The Loner and Superficial Friendships

Friendships are the source of a great part of an adolescent's image of himself. His status within a peer group as well as the status of his friendships accrue to how he is viewed by his peers. Observations of transactions within peer groups have shown that the friendship patterns can predict whether the member will have an active or passive social relationship in the future. An adolescent is either someone's acquaintance, someone's friend, someone's closest friend, and sometimes all of them at once. There is often a great deal of confusion over exactly where the adolescent belongs and why they are part of a certain subgroup. This confusion produces a great deal of tension which expresses itself in gossip, humor, long discussion/dialogues (bull-sessions), and indirect forms of aggression and teasing. The egocentricity of the age, noted above, tends to make the individual feel he is "center stage" and everyone is talking about him. Thus, the individual often reacts to the group's various means of reducing tension with further anxiety and fears of being rejected by the peer group or his close friends. These fears may be realistic or not (La Gaipa, 1979).

Some adolescents react to the excess of tension, fear and anxiety by withdrawing from intimate relationships and being content with superficial ones; others become cynical about friendship. Both reactions will lead to loneliness and frustration in terms of social relationships. This, in turn, may have a destructive effect on the adolescent's development and identity formation, both at this stage and later on.

Although our interviews indicated that honesty and credibility were the values adolescents, especially girls, held of the highest importance in a friendship, many adolescents have a low expectation of actually finding these qualities. They are particularly afraid of exposing themselves and being found wanting. Boys attempt to control their behavior, to appear composed and self-assured, "cool." This role playing is meant to avoid vulnerability, but actually blocks spontaneity and sincerity. Thus, an adolescent boy may find himself having only superficial relationships.

Loneliness may not arise simply from an adolescent's fear of self-disclosure and subsequent judging, out of "choice," but may also arise from social rejection. Research has shown that certain types of personalities are popular with their peers: adolescents perceived as tolerant, flexible, likable, with a sense of humor, always in a good mood, behave "naturally," self assured without being arrogant, who show initiative in social activities, etc. Adolescents who are not popular are perceived as lacking in self assurance, vulnerable, nervous, shy, egocentric. Many adolescents who are "not popular" socially actually do have friends and are satisfied with their relationships. However, many adolescents lack satisfying friendships. Therefore, it is necessary not only to help such adolescents develop the skills and abilities to make friends but also to make other adolescents aware of the existence of lonely individuals and develop their ability to reach out and help them.

Another reason for some adolescents' difficulty in forming and maintaining friendships is the "storm and stress" maturation pattern characterized by frequent bouts of depression. Such individuals find themselves in a situation where they need friends and the support they can supply, but at the same time they have a hard time making friends and/or maintaining an intimate relationship.

High Expectations of Friends; Inflexibility in Friendship

Evidence points to adolescents' deep disappointment with friends in certain cases. A study by Kon and Losenkov (1978) conducted in the Soviet Union indicated that few adolescents expressed satisfaction with their friendships. They report that when adolescents were asked the question, "How often, in your opinion, does one find true friendship among kids your age?" a large percentage of the respondents replied that it was very rare.

The same study produced several other interesting findings:

1. Girls of all ages rate friendship lower than do boys, apparently because the level of their expectations is higher than that of the boys.

2. The proportion of optimistic answers given by boys declines as the age increases.

3. The gap between boys and girls is greatest in the age range of 14-16, and the feeling that true friendship is very rare is much more prevalent among girls.

Since there have been no other similar studies, it is difficult to determine the extent to which these findings are universal. Discussions with adolescents have indicated that most idealize friendship and friends and have such high expectations that only few could possible fulfill them. Many adolescents expect their friends never to disappoint them, to know everything about them, to remain their friend for life, to be their friend exclusively, etc. Such inflexibility and high expectations inevitably lead to disillusionment with friends and an inability to enjoy a variety of friends, friendship of varying degrees of intensity and various forms of relationships.

As the adolescent matures he attains a social perspective which enables him to understand the complexity of friendship and realize that friends are not always available and at your service. In addition he becomes more able to forgo the exclusive aspect to the relationship and can adapt to the friend's needs for parallel heterosexual relationships.

Developmental Incompatibility Among Friends

Adolescents differ widely in their needs for interaction: at times some need only a few friends, while others need many; others maintain their friendships by means of a few hours of social contact a week, whereas others, particularly girls, must have hours of daily contact with their friends, either in person or on the telephone. The wide variation between adolescents in terms of the depth of self-disclosure they are willing to undertake and their expectations of friends makes it imperative that group leaders beware of stereotypical conceptualizing with regard to the scope and depth of a "meaningful relationship." When they intervene, they must be careful not to attach negative labels or urge the individuals beyond the involvement level set to protect them from loneliness.

Support provided by having friends lessens anxiety; however, having friends also causes anxiety: an individual may transfer his anxiety, related to an experience his friend has not been part of, to his friend; his anxiety may be increased as he attempts to prevent the friend from doing something viewed as undesirable; he may even present reality as more threatening than it is in order to increase the friend's appreciation of his support, etc. Studies of anxiety have shown that friendship seems to serve as a factor which increases anxiety for girls more than for boys. It would seem that this is because friendship among girls is more emotionally-focused whereas among boys it tend to be task-oriented.

Another area of development incompatibility has to do with the emotional and social development of the friends. Friendship is often a very intense relationship, a union of two individuals into one ego in which one of the friends is usually dominant. Sometimes, one of the friends has progressed sufficiently in his identity-formation to be able to differentiate himself from the other and begins to function within his own personality definition. The friend who is not yet ready for differentiation and change expects him to remain constant and feels hurt and betrayed and does not understand why he has been "deserted." This may also come about simply due to fluctuations in the various needs on which friendships are based. Thus, an old friend, which had been abandoned as the need he filled ebbed, may be reinstated and an ongoing friendship will be suddenly ended. Although such fluctuations are simply expressions of the individual's internal need for change, they may cause the friend disappointment and distress.

Another aspect of developmental incompatibility occurs when one of the friends is ready for interaction with members of the opposite sex or has greater success than the other in certain areas. The friend left out feels jealous, disappointed, neglected, lonely and worthless. This situation may not only have an adverse effect on the friendship, but it may even cause the friends to break up even though that may be the last thing they want to happen. The changes which have occurred in their relationship as the result of the new situation have created a conflict with which neither party is able to cope. In the case of a new interaction with a member of the opposite sex an additional factor causes problems for the friends: the change from a twosome to a threesome. An alignment of three is fundamentally different from an alignment of two; it requires maintaining an equilibrium between three entities with different traits, needs and reaction patterns.

Sometimes individuals feel guilty about wishing to break off a relationship which no longer satisfies them. The fear of hurting and disappointing the other makes it difficult to call an end to the relationship. Therefore, it is necessary to teach adolescents to deal actively with such situations.

Summary

Interviews and work with PPS groups have revealed five salient features around which difficulties with friendship seem to revolve:

1. **A preoccupation with identity-formation and meeting personal needs**. The business of identity-formation and dealing with personal needs including differentiation from parents, gaining status within peer contexts, forming relationships with members of the opposite sex is all-consuming. In many cases they are simply not ready to give, to fulfill someone else's needs; they are not ripe for a friendship involving reciprocity. Some adolescents may reach the stage sooner than their fellows; however, they reach the stage of forming relationships with members of the opposite sex and new problems develop, arising from this new set of needs.

2. **A lack of social perspective**. Selman (1980) points out that only at the age of 15-16 that social cognition reaches a level at which the individual is ready to perceive and consider the complexity of the friend's personality including perception of past, present and future needs and hopes. Most of friendship formation takes place before such

a level of social perspective is reached and seems to be the source for the oft-repeated complaint that their friends do not really understand them, don't consider their needs, don't allow them to be themselves, etc.

3. **Interference from adolescent egocentricity.** Elkind's (1967) description of adolescent egocentricity finds reflection in the complaints recorded that one or both parties of a relationship behave "as if only he existed," or "as if he were the center of the universe," or "as if he were unique," or "as if he were the only one with problems," etc.

4. **The bond with parents**. Although part of the main business of adolescence is differentiation from parents, the adolescent carries his internalized bond with him into his friendships. Our work with PPS groups and interviews has indicated that instead of replacing that bond, friends complement it. Unlike the suppositions of many researchers, although adolescents need friends and peer groups, neither of the two relationships serves as a substitute for their parents. Indeed, there are times when parental behavior irritates the youth, he will find solace with his friend; on the other hand, if the friend's behavior bothers him, he will seek relief in a different context-peer group, family, etc.

5. **General instability and change**. Adolescence is characterized by processes of reorientation, rapid change and uncertainty. Misunderstandings, frustration, mutual recriminations, dissolutions of friendships, and desires to renew friendships all come about as a result of the mixture of childhood primitiveness, the instability characteristic of adolescence and indecision due to the incompatibility between cognitive patterns left over from childhood and alternatives represented by peers, significant others and the mass media. Difficulties and conflicts are a natural occurrence and often require little more than positive support. Such support may also help many adolescents in shaping friendships, maintaining friendships and finally breaking off unwanted friendships. We will discuss this further in the following section.

More Explanations for Crises in Friendship Development: Positive and Negative

*   As described above, adolescent friendships, whether they develop suddenly or gradually, are linked to the fulfilling identity-formation and coping ability needs. At certain points and within certain contexts an adolescent needs someone and pulls him into a friendship (or is acted upon by another). Eventually, however, the needs of a friend from one social alignment may conflict with the needs of a friend in another (e.g., school vs. youth group, study alignment vs. leisure alignment, sexual identity vs. professional identity). At this point the conflict overpowers the need fulfillment.

* Sometimes the adolescent doesn't choose his friend, but rather is "impelled" by inner needs towards certain types of people. Although impelled toward this relationship, those very needs that are involved disrupt the development of the relationship. Douvan and Adelson (1966) note that friendships are based to a great extent on narcissism, identification and projection, all of which are problematic developmental processes. If an adolescent is too narcissistic (self-centered, self-loving), he will be over sensitive to rejection and will be afraid of surrendering himself completely to friendship demands; furthermore, he may be unable to be sensitive to the needs of others and be unprepared to fulfill the friend's expectations. An attraction to certain types of friends resulting from a quest for identity may undermine whatever differentiation and identity formation already achieved. Projection dominating a friendship context may result in the feeling that one party is trying to dominate the other or dictate the fulfillment of only his needs. Balancing these problematic areas is the fear of social isolation and the need for differentiation from one's parents. These forces serve to strengthen friendship bonds in the face of the disturbing or inhibiting factors described above.

* The source of the initial friendship tie often lies in a response rather than as a result of examination of positive significance through experience. A needs a friend-he is in the midst of a crisis having just broken up with his best friend, he is having a fight with his parents, he doesn't know anyone in the class, or B offers him high status in a group he wants to join, etc. B responds because of similar needs. The friendship was formed in the wake of their seeking support from each other and ultimately does not include a factor of reciprocity.

Therefore, experience together may reveal deeper incompatibilities and one of the parties may sooner or later, actively or passively, annul the friendship.

* A considerable number of relationships are based on sexual-erotic or aggressive impulses. The adolescent may be unable to exercise necessary self-control or have access to stabilizing guidance or other means of control and find himself in situations of conflict between his needs and those of his friend. The result may be the breakup of the friendship.

* Sometimes the needs on which a friendship is based arise out of a developmental stage rather than out of the need for a reciprocal relationship. Interviews revealed that a larger number of friendships than we expected seemed to be expressions of this factor, especially as it related to the need for someone to listen. Numerous adolescents were involved in episodes of self-expression, talking, playacting, etc. where the friends were his audience. The friends may have the need to be an audience or may simply be willing to play audience for him. There is a varying degree of awareness of this need. The adolescent may say, "I want someone to listen to me" or "My brain is so full of ideas/ my heart is so full of love/sadness/worry, I must let it out to someone." Sometimes the process is quite unconscious. Although the description may be "We are the kind of friends who tell each other everything," examples of interaction often reveals monologues rather than dialogues. Eventually, dissatisfaction with this state of affairs brings about the break-up of the friendship.

When a friendship succeeds in meeting certain needs-free him from a situation (e.g., social isolation in class), change a conceptualizing (e.g., I thought no one liked me because I was black), help him develop a social skill (e.g., learn to dance, get a girl/boyfriend)-that very success can bring about the end of the friendship.

Once they had accomplished whatever was represented by those particular needs, they felt ready to go on to a new stage and new types of friends. The old friendship was no longer satisfying. In effect, the friendship was a mediating factor which served to prepare them for a higher level of social perception or interpersonal relationships.

The reaction of the individuals towards this outgrowing of old friendships is often ambivalent; often the friendship is suddenly ended with an expression like "I've had it with him."

The factors described above, which are by no means a complete listing, contribute to the rapid development within adolescent friendships. A friendship often seems like a strange coalition of two very disparate individuals; the important question in such cases would seem to be why the friendship began in the first place rather than why did it end. We would assert that, just like such unlikely coalitions in adult life, it arose out of the need for support by one or both parties and is neither random nor inexplicable at all.

Occasionally parties of a friendship seem ideally compatible. They are so well-suited to each other that it would seem the friendship would last forever. Suddenly, unexpectedly, the friends break up. When discussing the situation with the friend who initiated the break-up, it comes out that the adolescent no longer wished such an idyllic arrangement. It felt like a sedative not a stimulant to him. He did not feel it was contributing to his development and maturation. He wanted something different, something challenging, stimulating, even a crisis which would, in effect, further his psycho-social development by undermining existing patterns and force him to reorient and integrate himself on a new and higher level of functioning.

5. Differences in Friendship Patterns: Boys and Girls

Conceptualizations and findings of research into this area reflects the starting point of the investigation, the focus of the study and variations in the interpretation of phenomena. Since we will deal with the subject more thoroughly in the next volume of this series, we will only cite examples which are important for the subject at hand: fellowship and friendship, particularly in unisexual instances.

Coleman's review of the nature of friendship in the various maturation stages (1980) indicates that the transition from unisexual to heterosexual friendships has not been studied very much. Moreover, the methodology employed in such studies has come under criticism. When considering the conclusions and evidence, we would recommend that it be remembered that patterns of friendship and significance are determined at least in part by the age variable. Since adolescence is characterized by rapid changes, it is important to remember that biological development and the development of a social IQ will affect perception, expectations and equality of the parties within the relationship. Blos (1962) represents the classic psychoanalytical approach and relies on clinical experience; Douvan and Adelson, in the United States, La Gaipa, in Canada, and Coleman, in England, are all empirical studies. We will conclude with generalizations based on our own work.

Blos points out that there are differences between boys and girls in rate and pattern of psychosexual development, particularly in early adolescence. Girls enter a period of rapid biological development earlier than boys. During the transition period, girls are more mature than boys: they study better, they have better social development, they have more capacity for introspection and more mature coping patterns. Boys fear their awakening sexuality and rebuff any attempt at physical or active contact on the part of members of the opposite sex: mothers, teachers or classmates.

At this stage a unisexual friendship provides boys with an opportunity for masculine identification and moral support, even at the price of a willingness to conform to the values and behavioral norms of the peer group or dominant friend. Unisexual friendship provides, girls more so than boys, a forum for mutual revelation of secrets and an approach to intimacy which borders on eroticism, even to the extent of experiencing caresses and masturbation.

Blos notes that early adolescence is a stage in friendship (still limited to the same sex) characterized by significant erotic nuances, some of them repressed, and some of them consciously experienced. Common masturbation, temporary homosexual tendencies and pursuits, mutual satisfaction, sharing aggressive feelings and forbidden acts, idealization, a sense of pleasure and elation in the presence of the beloved friend-all these are experiences which clearly demonstrate the narcissistic choice of the beloved object.

Douvan and Adelson (1966) examined friendship in three periods: Latency (age 11-13), also known as "Early Adolescence", Mid-Adolescence (age 14-16), and Late Adolescence (age 17 and over). Although their study, influenced by psychodynamic concepts, deals only with girls, it is one of the most fundamental in the field. Other studies can provide complementary material.

Early Adolescence (11-13)

Erikson notes (1950) that this period is characterized by diligence and development of general skills. The adolescent is more preoccupied with the external, material world than with his inner world. Friendships center around activity-what one can do with a friend and what the individual experiences while with the friend rather than on the friend himself. Although the friend serves as a frame of reference and comparison, there is no real interest in his character. Friends are judged and chosen according to superficial, external criteria: what can she do for me, how cooperative is she, is she nice, etc. The aim is to find a friend whose personality will not present a disturbance in common activity. The greatest commitment of the individual is still to her family, but as she grows and develops, she shows greater interest in the qualities and personality of her friend who eventually assumes the central frame of reference.

Mid-Adolescence (14-16)

Biological and emotional changes that adolescents undergo impel them away from family towards extra-familial friendships and intimate relationships. The friend's superficial qualities are less important now and deeper character traits assume a more central role. She wants to find a friend whom she can trust, who will understand and support her. She wants a friend who is sensitive to another's needs. The emphasis, unlike during early and late adolescence, is on security offered by the relationship-a friend who will be loyal and who can be depended upon in emotional crises. She also wants a friend who will be a reflection of herself. She will be able, with her friend's help, to deal with her heightened sexual impulses, to seek evaluation of her own development, to consolidate her identity. The emphasis on loyalty and security reflects the basic fear of this stage of adolescence: social isolation.

Late Adolescence (17 and up)

Friendship is beginning to have a more mature and tranquil character. The adolescent feels more comfortable with herself; she has developed biologically; she has developed a social perspective; she is making progress in her self-definition and sense of personal identity.

Friendship is no longer merely an arena for escape and encouragement. Friendship is based on a more profound understanding of the complexity endemic to the relationship as well as to the friend; the emphasis is on sharing experiences and events. There is a growing capacity to tolerate individual differences and recognize the other's capabilities. Early adolescent girls preferred friends older than themselves whereas late adolescents prefer friends of the same age or even younger.

Summary of Differences between Boys and Girls

Early adolescence friendship focuses around activity rather than interaction between the friends (including depth of relationship, reciprocity, emotional investment). Late adolescence friendship is more tranquil. This comes in part from the fact that late adolescents are able to consider more than their own personal needs, they can take note of the other's personality, areas of interest, uniqueness, and contribution to the overall friendship. It also stems from the fact that heterosexual relationships assume greater importance at this point and there is reduced emotional investment in unisexual relationships.

Coleman (1980) examined attitudes to friendship among boys and girls in the same age range. He discovered that the sense of insecurity and fear of rejection was strongest around the age of 15 which corresponds to the stage of Mid-Adolescence discussed above. Girls tend to feel greater anxiety and tension in friendship and over the possibility of rejection than boys throughout adolescence. This might reflect the greater emotionality and dependence on interpersonal relationship observed among girls.

Bigelow and La Gaipa (1980) reviewed various studies and publications and concluded that, in general, there were no substantial differences between boys and girls in their concept of friendship until adolescence, except that girls described their expectations of "a good friend" in more global and affective terms. The major difference that does arise during adolescence is that girls worry more about loyalty and mutual commitment of their "best friends" than do boys. 75% of late adolescent girls named these two criteria as important compared to 52% of boys. Of especial concern was confidentiality concerning intimate information. Loyalty and commitment were issues in terms of the breakup of friendships. 47% of early adolescent girls compared with 21% of the boys and 47% of late-adolescent girls as opposed to 32% of the boys cited these criteria when discussing the breakup of their friendships.

There were differences between the sexes with regard to revelation of intimate information; however, they weren't as pronounced as might have been expected: Early adolescent girls emphasized intimacy more than boys (23-9%); in late adolescence the emphasis was 60-40%. There were no substantial differences between the sexes in terms of this factor as a cause for disrupting friendship.

Interviews and PPS group experience, reflecting a variety of socio-economic as well of cultural backgrounds, in the United States and Israel, have pointed to five salient points:

1. Girls focus on affective areas; boys focus on enjoying shared tasks. Consistently the girls' expectations of a relationship are focused on affective areas; boys look at the enjoyment of shared activity.

2. Although crises in friendships and a high turnover rate are the same, causes are different. Girls are disappointed in friendships which do not meet their expectations of reciprocity, of shared confidences, of support, etc. Their high expectations mean their disappointment is severe. Boys change interests, tasks and activities and thus change the composition of their friendships.

3. Intimacy is more of an issue for girls. Beginning with eighth grade adolescent girls tend to reveal themselves more in intimate matters: family, friends, falling in love with a teacher, private difficulties, etc. Therefore, they are more anxious when a friendship breaks up or threatens to break up-they have invested more in the friendship and they fear that the ex-friend may divulge the secrets they know.

4. Complications of early physical maturation. Because of their earlier biological-sexual maturation, girls become interested in hetero-sexual relationships earlier than boys. This causes a conflict between the intra-sexual and inter-sexual friendship relationships and raises anxieties related to disloyalty and disclosure of confidences. Although this can begin in early adolescence, it becomes even more notable in late adolescence. Because of the gap in the biological-sexual development of their age-mates, girls may form relationships with boys older than themselves, in higher grades, in college and even those who are in the work world. They enter new experiences-become members of more mature peer groups, experience sexual relations-and the significance of their relationship with boys in their class changes and the gap grows wider.

5. Late Adolescent Differences in Perception and Expectations. In late adolescence the differences in perception and expectations of friendship reflects a difference in fashioning a personal identity and future life-style. Boys speak of maturation tasks: career, college, politics, the army and view friendship as an element of support, cognitive, affective or instrumental, in dealing with those tasks. Girls, on the other hand, focus on patterns of interpersonal relationships like intimacy and commitment, and reflect, either directly or indirectly, to the subject of marriage and choice of spouse.

Coleman (1980) suggests that the difference in socialization of the two sexes legitimizes girls to express their feelings and concentrate on the interaction between themselves and their friends while boys must stress achievement in tasks, involving competition between themselves and their friends. Douvan & Adelson agree, maintaining further that the girl's future role of wife and mother requires her to develop qualities like sensitivity, warmth, tact and empathy-all qualities which are important in establishing and maintaining friendship as well. Boys, on the other hand, are socialized to act and achieve which requires assertiveness, independence and competitiveness.

Helen Deutsch (1947), and other classical psychoanalytical theoreticians, deal with the fundamentally different psychosexual tasks for boys and girls. All adolescents, they note, must sever their old object relationships (parents as the objects) in favor of new ones (friend or spouse as the new objects). The development of sexual drives means that they must transfer such feelings from the parents to appropriate objects. The difference between the sexes has to do with the physical sexual development itself. Boys find it easier to define and understand their sexuality. Their experiences are direct, clear, more legitimate and generally unequivocal. Girls' sexuality is not so straightforward and based on internal, physical processes. She needs intimate friendships which will help her clarify her sexuality. An adolescent girl defines her identity by means of a synthesis of erotic and interpersonal aspects while an adolescent boy defines his identity by means of qualities such as autonomy, assertiveness and achievement. The nature of friendships of boys and girls reflects this basic difference: boys tend to establish groups or gangs based on competitive activity; girls prefer groups which divide up into more intimate two- or threesomes.

Furthermore, the difference is reflected in motives for friendship. Boys seek less intimacy than do girls and depend on their groups more for support and a source of guidance. In early adolescence boys chose concrete attributes similar to those chosen by preadolescent girls as criteria for choosing friends or that which makes someone popular. They were more interested in common activity than the friend's personality, commitment to the relationship or understanding and emotional support provided. They did not emphasize sensitivity or empathy and were much less preoccupied with the various aspects of the relationship itself. They were interested in the fact of belonging to a group with its norms and standards and feared rejection because of nonconformity to the group. Girls, on the other hand, expressed the need for love as a primary motive for friendship with the concomitant fear of the loss of love as a primary source of anxiety.

Lever (1976) relates the differences between boys and girls to the difference between girls' and boys' games. Boys are active in games with clear-cut frameworks with well-defined roles and which are based on rules similar to the rules of a structured societal group (football has clear-cut rules, well-defined roles, etc.). Boys are playing games which are structured in terms of developing skills at coping with and performing tasks within social systems. Girls, however, play games which are aimed more at forming interpersonal relationships, maintaining social relationships and providing opportunities for social interaction (hopscotch, jump rope). There is less emphasis on regulation and competitiveness, which characterizes boys' games and adult men's lives.

Lipman-Blummen (1975), a sociologist and a feminist, discusses the social and economic influences which have caused men to value masculine society more highly than feminine society. She claims that throughout history most of the sources of power, status and economic activity have been concentrated in the hands of men. Therefore, boys (and later on, men) form more powerful groups than do girls. Boys' groups concentrate less on interpersonal interaction and more on various tasks-of pleasure, work, money, etc.

Although feminine friendship is marked by intimacy and greater depth, it is subject to special difficulties. Precisely because of the greater closeness between parties of such relationships, the level of anxiety is much higher for girls than for boys. Tension, rejection-fears, jealousy and conflict are more frequent in adolescent girl friendships than in those between adolescent boys. The very mode of the girls' relationships-great intimacy and intense dependence-makes it difficult for girls to maintain simultaneous friendships of varying natures and degrees of intensity with various friends for different purposes. Any relationship which is less than very intimate seems to be inferior and less satisfying. Lipman-Blummen ascribes female dissatisfaction with their relationships with other women to the fact that most social power-political and economic-is concentrated in the hands of men. Therefore, she notes, women gain status by being included in the company of men and not in the company of other women. Although this describes an adult context, it may be assumed the origin of this friendship pattern lies in friendship patterns of adolescents. It would be important for adolescents to deal with this problem and consider its significance for them.

PPS Groups and the Significance of Differences between the Sexes

As early as Early Adolescence (12-13) it is possible to help adolescents develop awareness of the fact that friendship promotes change and growth and can be consciously fashioned and used for self-development purposes. This awareness occurs in different dimensions and on different levels. The adolescent can develop himself through self-awareness: of his own development, attributes, vulnerabilities in certain areas; at the same time he can become aware of others: observe them, try to understand them and their outlook on life.

Once the awareness of the possibility of conscious fashioning of friendship is established, it will expand to include certain desirable criteria for friendship. The child's original concept of friendship as mutual service (helping with homework, playing together, defending one another against an outsider's violence, etc.) will broaden to include the idea of friendship as a complement to developmental needs: dealing with narcissism, projection, identification and aggressiveness.

Because of the varied, complex quality of the needs, the intervention process must be different for different types of adolescents. For example, girls at this age have a more rapid rate of social and biological development and are more sensitive to the potential significance of friendship; they tend to fashion relationships which are both more extensive and more profound. Although most friendships are based on similarities between friends, complementary dissimilarities play an important role as well. This process may be compared to later patterns in choosing a spouse and establishing a family. Therefore, it is important that during the support process the adolescents should be assured of the legitimacy of systematic selectivity. They should be encouraged to understand and serve the needs of their friends and at the same time they should be aware of their right and responsibility that at every stage of development they have made the most of the significance of the friendship.

A PPS group should encourage the clarification of the various, age-appropriate friendship patterns. Therefore, girls from early adolescence would seek support in addition to the support they receive from their family; at a later stage, age 14-16, they would seek something deeper and more problematic. Their emerging sexuality and differentiation from parents engender greater expectations of peer group and close friends; friendships are more intensive and more intimate and concomitantly more anxiety-provoking and potentially painful. Statements like: "I told her everything; I relied on her and now everything has been wrecked" tells the whole story: the girl confided in her friend, relying on her to keep her secret, and now she fears the secret will be used against her by other friends or "enemies." Girls at this stage are no longer satisfied by friendships consisting of shared activity and mutual service. They want a friend in whom they can confide, who can be trusted, who will keep their secrets, who is sensitive. Girls want to share secrets; they want a friend who will give them confidence, loyalty and emotional as well as practical support. In many cases they invest so much in a friendship that the loss of the friend actually amounts to four separate losses:
* loss of part of themselves (the aspect of identity-shaping which required complementing by the other)
* possible loss of intimate secrets
* loss of a source of emotional and practical support

* loss of faith in others

Adults, too, have faced such a loss. However, for the most part, adults do not feel it as a catastrophe. For someone who has not experienced intimacy on such a level of intensity, the breakup of such a relationship presents a very painful emotional conundrum. Not only does the adolescent feel exposed and betrayed, but he is also afraid of blackmail. Perhaps surprisingly adolescent girls often form new friendships shortly after the termination of the old ones. It would appear that the intense need for intimate friendship provides a quick cure from the bad effects of the breakup of a former friendship.

Conclusions

There are four central problems in friendship formation at this stage of development:

Sexuality

The search for a personal identity and self esteem

Membership in subgroups (cliques)

Establishing relationships with members of the opposite sex

Sexuality is a central subject in discussions revolving around self-disclosure. Many times girls refer to other girls as "loose," "bad" or even "promiscuous" (she sleeps around, she's a punchboard) as a means of ventilating their sexual needs through projection. This is particularly true for girls who are not ready to become sexually active themselves. At this stage the adolescent girl views herself and her friends as members of the group of "good girls" as opposed to the others who are "bad girls."

The second central problem revolves around personal identity and self esteem. At this stage the girl may lose touch with her identity and doubt her self-worth. She needs peers to help define her and respect her. Another way to gain respect and support is to become part of a clique, which is a small group based on personal loyalty and confidentiality, closed to outsiders and highly supportive of its members. As much as a clique will help its members, its very exclusivity and closed quality represent a problem for girls on the outside.

Finally, when girls begin to establish relationships with boys, a whole new crop of problems surface. Such relationships promise much and demand much in terms of feelings, learning and coping. It is at this point that the girl establishes her pattern of relating with boys.

PPS group discussion and interviews revealed another aspect of concern in the boy-girl relationships: that of social ethics. This includes the extent of self-disclosure, willingness to engage in sexual activity, the nature of the boy's continued relationship with his male friends, the extent of the boy's discretion in terms of talking about his experiences with his girlfriend to his male friends, and the girl's fear of rejection. This latter fear includes the fear that the boy will prefer another girl to her and will reveal her secrets and the nature of their relationship. In this area there is a pronounced gap between boys and girls. Many girls, who have matured physically much faster than the boys, seem like women when compared to their age-mates. Sometimes the boys perceive them as sexually threatening; sometimes they view them as outsiders because their social and emotional world is often outside their age-group-they may mix with boys from upper grades or even from outside the school context.

Advanced adolescence-the last two years of high school, ages 16-18-tends to be more tranquil and settled. Boys have caught up with the girls in their physical development and have both uni- and heterosexual friendships. Most boys have had a direct relationship with a girl although most have not experienced full sexual relations. A large number of girls in class, and in the various peer groups, have had relationships with older boys and even some of those who have not become sexually active speak about the subject as if they have. Experience in relationships with boys seems to have a tranquilizing effect on relationships between the girls; it is as though all the energy which had heretofore been invested in the relationship between the girls is now being channeled into heterosexual relationships. Despite the tranquility, relationships between girls now reach a higher level of understanding of mutual needs, of mutual support, of willingness to reveal oneself and particularly of willingness to accept the unique personality and variations in moods of the other party. Now, we see that friendships simply end instead of breaking up because of conflicts. Interviews and discussions in PPS groups contain fewer complaints expressing doubts about someone's loyalty and more descriptions of the friend's qualities as a person. Stereotypical labels gradually disappear.

Chapter Five: Social Organizations: Their Influence on the Development of Friendship

Schools and other socializing institutions were referred to in our model of the systematic conceptualizing of friendship and fellowship development as factors promoting or inhibiting such development. Educational institutions affect the process in different ways, some of which are clear and conscious and result from values and ideational or organizational needs of the policy-makers. Others are unconscious but stem as side-effects of solutions for other problems. It is important for all those involved: policy makers like the Minister of Education, mayors, legislators, and bureaucrats, those in executive positions like in the Department of Education, in the School Districts, in the municipalities and in the schools themselves, counselors and teachers who mediate between policy-makers and those affected by the policies, and finally, the adolescents themselves to understand how the educational system influences friendship development and be aware of the various factors involved.

The school as an institution constitutes one factor in and of itself. In the school there are a combination of factors, each of which contributes its relative share to the process. When we refer to schools, we are referring in the main to "day schools" rather than boarding schools. Approximately 85% of the adolescent student population attend day schools in Israel.

1. Geographic Proximity

A primary influential factor is physical proximity. Without physical proximity there would be virtually no possibility for a person to be influenced by others or to develop a relationship with them. Examples of effecting proximity are the personal, political and administrative decisions about coeducation and Educational Reform of 1968 whereby children from various ethnic and social backgrounds were integrated into the same schools. This reform was actively and passively opposed by some mayors, leaders of religious education, parents and others. The opposition was indicative of opposition to proximity with certain groups. Occasionally, educational reform such as this had the opposite effect-busing children out of their neighborhoods to give them proximity to other groups and preventing proximity in their home neighborhoods and schools. Decision-makers determined, by drawing their maps of the new school districts, which children would associate with which children. All the evidence shows that attendance in a school with a mixed population, particularly over a long period of time, affects the child's opportunities for meeting children from other backgrounds. Thus, busing children to and from schools in different neighborhoods influenced directly the possibility of developing friendships between certain groups.

2. Organizational and Structural Factors

The institutional organization, implementing political and administrative decision, is the second factor influencing friendship development patterns. The structure of the school: homogeneous vs. heterogeneous classes, streaming, differentiation, majors, electives affect the opportunities for forming friendships.

Studies of the ways in which institutional organization and modes of institutional activity affect friendships begin with early childhood (Charlesworth & Hartup, 1967; Asher, Oden & Gottman, 1977; Corsero, 1981). Hallinan (1976) studied the effect of institutional organization on mutuality vs. asymmetry and the degree of stability in the choice of friends in the fourth grade. Bossert (1979) describes the effect of the seating arrangement in elementary schools on child groupings in playground games. Byrne (1961) notes how the seating arrangement affects the choice of friends even at the college level.

There is a great deal of evidence to support the contention that the lack of friendship stability, described in previous chapters in terms of developing social perspective and differing stages in identity formation, is related to the many changes in classroom composition from one year to another, and in some institutions, from one term to another. Epstein (1983) reports various studies confirming that the short duration of friendships results from changes in the composition of the learning units (classes, aptitude groups, majors, etc.).

Israel's educational system takes students after completing elementary school (sixth grade) and transfers them to a regional junior high school which may require busing out of the geographical area. The seventh grade is organized around homerooms and some of the subjects are further broken down into aptitude groups. Eight grade sees an increase in subjects with aptitude groups and the groups themselves change their composition. Some students leave the school in ninth grade, attending a vocational, agricultural, special, experimental or simply a four-year high school which begins in the ninth grade. Tenth grade means moving up to a senior high school and a new set of class mates, new groups with new aptitude groups. Differentiation can occur within the school with some of the students moving into academic tracks and others into vocational. Eleventh grade sees a further differentiation and reorganization. Children who transfer out of the school face the problem of a lack of friends as well as adaptation to the new educational requirements; children who remain behind often find themselves having to establish intimate relationships with someone else.

It is possible to organize classes and aptitude groups on the basis of various criteria, including ability, achievement, socially and ethnically balanced constitution, geographically proportional representation, etc. At the same time that this influences the formation of new groupings, it breaks up former groupings and friendships.

Organizational changes can affect the development of various age groups in other ways. For example boys constitute only 40% of the student population in academic secondary schools; vocational schools differ in their majority depending on the subject: only 25-30% of the students in agricultural high schools are girls, schools concentrating on electronics and computers are highly male, and schools concentrating on fashion, cooking and clerical/business are highly female. The comprehensive school would be the most heterogeneous in terms of offering opportunities for friendships, whereas the selective, differentiated secondary school divides its students into aptitude groups which confer different status on members of different groups. The achievement criteria is already determining the composition of junior high school groups at the time when heterosexual friendships are being formed.

3. The School's Social and Educational Climate

The third factor in friendship formation is the learning pattern within the school system. Most schools are organized around some balance between cooperation and competition between students. Some institutions emphasize the value of group cooperation, while others emphasize competitive individual achievement. This emphasis manifests itself in organization patterns, social climate, learning assignments and methods of evaluation. An outstanding example of an emphasis on cooperation in the Israeli educational system is to be found in the schools of the kibbutz movement. These schools oppose differentiation according to ability and evaluation tests and have attempted to institute cooperative learning by means of projects and norms of mutual responsibility even at the cost of marked underachievement. An example of the opposite extreme can be found in various highly selective secondary schools which operate on the principle of differentiation and selection for all classes. Not all students are accepted into the school and those who are are organized into homogeneous classes and are under constant threat of expulsion if they fail to live up to certain academic standards.

In Manor's study of the influence of the social-educational climate in 40 schools (1983), it was clear how some types of schools opened up developmental possibilities which had been blocked by other schools. Epstein (1983) discusses the influence of the organization of study patterns and reward systems on social involvement and fellowship. More specifically Hallinan (1976) found that in open study classes there were fewer isolated children and fewer "stars." French (1977) and La Gaipa (1981) described how a pattern of cooperation and help of the weaker students by the stronger, over the long term, had an adverse effect on potential friendships between the helpers and the helped. It would seem that the long term helping program created dependence on the part of the recipients of support and harmed their chances of being perceived as worthy of friendship. Cohen (1980) demonstrated students with unequal status, no matter on what criteria it was based, will not cooperate unless the teacher finds a way to change the study patterns so that low status students will have a chance to participate in some high status activities. Cooperation seems to depend on equal status within the student body and a situation revolving around low vs. high status pupils will prevent cooperation.

Chapter Six: Loneliness

1. The Scope of the Problem

Keeping in mind the description of the importance of interpersonal reciprocal relationship at various stages in development, the questions arise: what proportion of the population has difficulty in interpersonal relations in general and in making friends in particular? How can this developmental deficiency be explained? What is the correlation between difficulty in making friends during childhood and adolescence and loneliness in adulthood? How does loneliness influence the biological and psycho-social state of the individual? How much do we actually know about loneliness as a subject in and of itself? Why has the subject not been raised in teacher-training or inservice courses and why has no program of studies been developed to deal with the problem?

Loneliness, like friendship, has been part of human experience throughout history, and humans encounter it throughout their lives. Philosophers, legislators for both tribal and universalistic religions, writers, poets have referred to loneliness in all ages as a fundamental human problem and have described it in the light of their own feelings, needs and ability to express themselves.

The fifties and sixties saw behavioral science discussions of loneliness: a painful, frightening, severe problem (Sullivan, 1953; Fromm-Reichman, 1959; Leiderman, 1969). However systematic research developed only in the seventies and consolidated in the eighties. Weiss (1973) saw loneliness as a chronic problem prevalent throughout society; Lynch (1977) saw statistical evidence of loneliness as a cause of declining physical health; Spitzberg and Cannary (1985) connect loneliness and depression, loneliness and a sense of social failure, loneliness and hostility, loneliness and alcoholism and drug abuse, suicide attempts and premature death. They conclude that lonely people view themselves as incapable of close interpersonal relationships and others view them similarly.

Estimation of the scope of the problem is quite difficult. Attitudes and expectations about feelings and behavior patterns, affected by value judgments on the part of both the subject and the researcher, do not tend to take into account differences in culture patterns, religion, ethnicity, and social class and tend to reflect norms of desirable behavior which may vary for children, men and women. In addition, evaluation tools and criteria and interpretations of findings also differ. Studies conducted in countries with an advanced stage of modernization-the United States, Canada and England-could be assumed to deal with similar social conditions vis a vis the individual. Even if there is no exact comparison, such evaluations can be utilized to encourage counselors, educators and others to examine the subject from within the realm of their own activity.

Our survey of research into the subject begins with studies about loneliness for adults and follow with studies about children and adolescents.

Bryand and Truber (1974) reported that 42% first year students at Oxford University had moderate to severe difficulties in social relations. Zimbardo (1977) found 42% of 2500 American college students were shy in the context of social relationships. Ishiyama (1984) reports on studies indicating that shyness characterizes approximately 40% of all Americans. Moreover, he found that those who were shy noted that their shyness was an obstacle to Social success and development of peer relations.

Shyness is not, of course, identical with loneliness. However, a positive correlation has been established between shyness in childhood or adolescence and loneliness. Cheek and Busch (1981) find a positive correlation between shyness and loneliness. Argyle (1981) uses a number of studies to enumerate some basic difficulties of young people, including anxiety in the face of interpersonal interaction (the most prominent), difficulties in forming relationships with the opposite sex and difficulties in making friends. Perlman and Peplau (1981) conclude that a quarter of the population in America may be categorized as "lonely."

2. The Causes of Loneliness: The Processes and Their Significance

The occurrence of loneliness is not a random accident. It develops like friendship and results from a system of interrelated causes. First and foremost is the accelerated development of modern society. The technological revolution destroyed the social structure of the village and town where the extended family, the religious community, the work place and the school were all interrelated. It is true that even in that society loneliness existed and there were lonely people. However, the uniformity of values, the population density, and the interrelation of all phases of life gave rise to values of involvement and a pattern of togetherness.

The technological revolution and the urbanization process separated the work place from the place of residence, channeled men and women to separate places of activity, created additional housing for nuclear families and individuals, and advanced the dispersion of various members of the family far beyond the boundaries of the community. These factors stimulated social mobility and led to a situation in which inhabitants of the same building sometimes found themselves leading lonely lives bound by the walls of their apartment.

Other components of modernization, such as secularization and democratization, have had their effect on loneliness. Modern societies convey the message that individualism and personal autonomy are the culmination of achievement. Starting with kindergarten, emphasis is placed on privacy and non-interference which may be interpreted as noninvolvement and lack of commitment to others, whether they are family members or fellow students and workers. Ambition for personal achievement, also fostered from an early age, often replaces friendship and reciprocity. There is a growing focus on the needs of the individual, which, when viewed positively, is referred to as self-realization, and when viewed negatively as the "Me Generation." Democratization, another aspect of concentration on the individual, produces expectations that each individual is equal to the next.

In many instances the expectations of self-realization and equality are not realized, giving rise to disillusionment, frustration and alienation. An alienated person, whether alienated in the sphere of politics, society, work or any group which he considers a social frame of reference, perceives himself as lonely.

Socializing institutions can also be the source of loneliness. As has been noted above, schools are bureaucratic entities, guided by criteria which are political, budgetary, organizational, etc. and often ignore the reality of the individual who may lose a feeling of social relationship, fellowship and friendship in the process, and end up feeling like a "cog in the wheel" and isolated.

Clinical psychologists, social psychologists and others connect loneliness with personality characteristics and evolving interpersonal situations. Such situations are created by the individual or result from transactions between himself and others.

Jones et al. (1981) points out that lonely people lack social skills and have difficulty in relationships with members of the opposite sex; moreover, they report general dissatisfaction with their efforts at courtship and making friends. The study points out that isolated people in situations of social intercourse are less aware of others' needs, show less response to the person with whom they are conversing and dwell more on themselves in the course of the conversation. This would seem to indicate they are self-centered. Moreover, isolated people tended to consider themselves low in social skills and in attractiveness although this did not always match others' opinions.

Check et al. (1985) revealed that people without social skills have preconceptions which led them to incorrect evaluations of various situations and in turn hindered social relations. Isolated people had negative opinions of others from whom they would have candidates for acquaintance and friendship. They express an exaggerated sensitivity to any slightly negative sign in others; that plus the tendency to interpret such signs incorrectly meant they reacted as if the other had hostile intentions.

We have a picture of a cycle of reactions: a lack of social skills within interpersonal interaction leads to a lack of self-confidence and hypersensitivity which leads to a negative, exaggerated interpretation of the potential friend's reactions and these misinterpreted reactions then serve as proof of a generalized hostility which in turn justifies remaining isolated.

Rubin (1982) ascertains that the fundamentals needed for the development and maintenance of friendship are established in nursery school and kindergarten. If these social skills are not acquired, the result may be regression, withdrawal and social isolation. As Check et al. (1985) correctly notes: loneliness is both the cause and the effect of the feelings and behavior of isolated people.

Spitzberg and Cannary (1985) have attempted to generalize about the causes of loneliness based on existing evidence. They claim that there is a cyclical reaction which fosters the condition of loneliness. Shyness and depression lead to the isolation of people who find it difficult to form friendships. These causes prevent achievement in an important area which might lead to positive changes in their situation. Their constant loneliness leads to an increase in anxiety and fear of situations which require interaction. Gradually, this situation leads to negative social experiences and a decline in the social skills which are vital in order to maintain an interpersonal interaction with significant others. The negative social experiences, in turn, further enhance the feeling of loneliness.

Spitzberg and Cannary explain this phenomenon using the theory of attribution which is the way people perceive things, label them and act accordingly. The theory of attribution looks at loneliness and focuses on three things: inner causes, stability of the situation and the capacity for control. Accordingly, a person may attribute his loneliness to intrinsic causes (such as un-attractiveness or lack of social skills) or to external causes (such as peers who show no personal interest or a limiting situation); to stable causes (the absence of opportunity to meet people in this sort of job) or to unstable causes (being new in the neighborhood, pressure at work, difficulties in another social alignment); finally, loneliness may be attributed to factors over which one has control (lack of effort at meeting suitable persons) or to factors over which one has no control (moving to new place, nobody suitable at work place).

3. Children Without Friends

Thus far we have reviewed the importance of friendship, beginning with childhood. We have noted that friends foster the development of social skills by providing the child with regular access to play groups; by enabling him to play a complex form of games; and by providing guidance and practice in areas such as cognitive development, sexual function, establishment of interpersonal relationships, and control of aggression. Friends also fulfill emotional functions by providing confidence and support in various social situations.

In view of the important and varied function which friendship has in childhood, it is worrying to note how many children lack friends. Studies show that despite the social change which has taken place since World War II, the number of children who are isolated in elementary school has not changed. Sociometric tests conducted in the classroom showed that 5-10% of all children were not chosen as a friend by any of their classmates.

In addition to the manifest unhappiness of such isolated children, it has emerged that friendless children tend to be expelled from school and are drawn into crime more often than others. Friendless children get no attention in the classroom or in the playground; they are isolated and often the teacher doesn't even pay them any attention. Thus, even when they need help, it is difficult for them to get it, due to the paucity of interactions in which they are involved. These children are, in a sense, excluded from any significant social contact despite their physical presence; their opinions do not count; their remarks are unheeded; they are forgotten and unnecessary. Thus, they lose their capacity for involvement, influence, and social supervision. Since they are ignored and isolated, these children do not enjoy a healthy pattern of activity. When their expectations for attention are not realized, their confidence and social perspective are undermined, and their judgment of interpersonal relations is narrowed and distorted.

Sociometric questionnaires indicate that friendless children are not homogeneous, but may be grouped into three general categories:

* withdrawn from the social scene
* disinterested in the social scene
* ineffective in social intercourse

"Withdrawn" children are characterized, in many cases, by the following: they lack vitality, they are physically weak, they are indifferent, they are often below average intelligence or do not utilize their abilities effectively; they don't care about their appearance and have sloppy work habits, they are uninterested in people, activities and events in the outside world, they lack inner curiosity and drive. In contrast to rowdy and aggressive children, withdrawn children are no trouble to others. Therefore, the symptoms indicating their lack of adjustment are not clearly evident. It is very important that parents and teachers be sensitive to discerning symptoms of withdrawal. The withdrawn child stays away from other children, remains by himself during recess or when other children engage in social activity. He does not participate in games and prefers to play by himself. He may prefer the company of children younger than himself and avoid the company of children his own age.

"Socially disinterested" children resemble withdrawn children in that they are not liked, or they make no effort at formal classroom activities. They are quiet and withdrawn, but more developed in their concern for their personality, their appearance, and their belongings. They have personal interests rather than social interests (such as music, art, science, hobbies, reading). These children are quiet and not interested in others.

"Socially ineffective" children attempt to gain attention. For instance, they may be noisy, rebellious, boastful. They are disruptive. They may annoy others or disrupt lessons; they are usually rejected by their classmates. Their reaction to rejection from their classmates is to try to overcome their social insecurity by repeated, unsuccessful, attempts to make friends.

There are several causes for the fact that children fail to make friends. These causes include a combination of personal characteristics (such as basic personality traits, appearance, family background) and situational factors (availability of peer groups, opportunities for friendship). In addition, a lack of social skills or some of their components will lead to isolation. Acquisition of a variety of social skills through observation, identification and imitation makes it possible for a child to deal more successfully with the problems of friendship.

The process of isolation and social withdrawal is sometimes viewed as a pattern of adjustment to tension. This pattern of adjustment develops by trial and error-the child tries various alternatives to lessen his tension (whose source may be either internal or external) until he reaches the most likely one: withdrawal from any further effort at making friends. However, such an escape from tension-arousing activities leads to a negative response on the part of other children which further encourages the withdrawal of the isolated child.

As long as the withdrawal is a reaction to real threats and to specific situations which sometimes develop at school, it may be considered a logical step. However, when it becomes a generalized pattern and the child begins avoiding any social interaction, the mechanism no longer serves its purpose and becomes harmful.

A child's avoidance of making friends may develop as a result of imitation of his parental model. Thus, if his parents occupy themselves in activities of an isolating nature (watching TV, reading, drinking) and have no contact with friends, the child has no model of making and maintaining friends to imitate.

A person's isolation may also be related to his parents' treatment of him as a child. Withdrawal (introverted behavior) may be related to parental rejection, behavior which does not convey a desire or motivation for establishing interaction. Such parents, through avoidance, or sometimes through punishment and harsh treatment of the child, create an unpleasant experience associated with relationships. This establishes the basis for the child's avoiding relationships later on. On the other hand, parents, who are loving and attentive to the child and his outside relationships and present a model of openness to relationships and experiences, arouse their child's need for relationships and experiences.

Psychoanalysis explains difficulty in making friends as an aspect of the flawed development of the child's normal object relationships. The mother-child relationship is the basis for normal integration and definition of the boundaries of the self. Based on this relationship, the child develops relationships with others. A flawed relationship may lead to asocial behavior and personality disturbance.

Asher and Renshaw (1981) offer a more general social explanation. They view any social interaction as requiring the capacity to participate and share experiences, to cooperate and communicate and to give and receive support. In addition, a child must, in the course of his development, acquire some general principles and concepts related to social interaction. He must know which specific behavior patterns constitute a certain behavioral continuum, which goals to set in any given situation, and he must be able to identify what effect he has on others. Children who have no friends appear to lack these skills.

4. Loneliness for Adolescents

Despite the importance of the subject, the number of studies dealing with loneliness in adolescence is quite limited. Sullivan (1953) is the outstanding theoretician in describing the intensity of feelings due to loneliness in preadolescents. He asserted that one of the maturation tasks in preadolescence and early adolescence is the ability to develop intimate interpersonal relationships with a friend of the same sex. The significance of such an experience is that for the first time in his life the child learns the meaning of mutuality by responding to the needs of a significant other. By means of this mutual relationships both parties not only gain pleasure and support, but also confirmation of their personal worth. The natural result of this development at the preadolescent stage is the development of readiness for pro-social behavior, i.e., a concern for the fate of others.

Manarino (1975) and Strickland (1981) found empirical support for Sullivan's assumptions concerning a positive correlation between the capacity for intimate friendship and a strong altruistic orientation.

Blos (1962, 1979) points out the process involved in the compulsion to differentiate from the parent of the opposite sex at the point when the adolescent's sexuality awakens and he reaches the oedipal stage simultaneous with understanding the intra-familial sexual taboo. This results in the maturation pattern called "storm and stress" which leads to the strengthening of the ego. Adolescents seek equilibrium in the support of their peers and usually find it in the form of friends. However, those who have difficulties in achieving differentiation from parents and lack social skills endure loneliness. Mahon (1983) found that loneliness is more intense in early adolescence than in later periods.

Erikson (1950, 1968) finds a polarity in each of Man's developmental stages and maintains that during adolescence this polarity is between determination of identity and confusion of identity. He defines loneliness and isolation as a negative developmental state, characterizing those who are unable to establish an intimate personal relationship based on mutual openness and mutual commitment. The salient difference between Sullivan and Erikson must be noted. Erikson viewed the fashioning of a personal identity as the task of adolescence and assumed that only those who had achieved this task were capable of intimacy. Sullivan, on the other hand, described intimate friendships between members of the same sex during preadolescence. These relationships were a precondition for personal-social identity fashioning and the establishment of mature intimate relationships with members of the opposite sex in adult life.

According to Elkind (1967) strong egocentricity in an adolescent combined with a lack of empathy and social skills, and an inability to acquire social perspective, may lead to loneliness. Williams (1983) maintains that adolescents feel on the one hand they should not be dependent on anyone and on the other hand they have not advanced far enough in the differentiation process and are still dependent on their parents. Loneliness and despair may develop as a result of the adolescent's feeling that he does not command enough support and cannot therefore establish any friendships. She attributes the problem to the gap between the needs and expectations which a person has of the rewards of friendship and his inability to receive support and reinforcement of his expectations.

Some point to social conditions in the family and society at large, that greatly aggravate the problems of adolescents including their sense of loneliness: the rising divorce-rate, mobility leading to frequent changing of homes and schools, confusion on the part of parents as to their parenting roles, etc. Some even attribute feelings of isolation to the structure of the school system with its transfer of early adolescents from a small, neighborhood environment to a larger, impersonal junior high school which is unfamiliar, competitive and less intimate.

Summary

Children of all ages need social skills which make it possible for them to cooperate, share and make friends with each other. Young children regard the children with whom they come into close contact, with whom they have positive interaction, and with whom they share material resources such as toys as friends. Older children establish friendships on the basis of mutual help and mutual sharing of thoughts, feelings and common interests. With older children friendship is based on understanding and loyalty rather than on positive interaction and close contact. Older children therefore particularly need skills which will enable them to identify common areas of interest; to express thoughts, ideas and feelings and to establish a climate of trust.

Research literature indicates that **it is possible to teach social skills required to make friends with one's age cohort** (Bigelow, 1977; Selman, 1981; Spivak and Shure, 1974).

Friendship is one of the focal areas in the development of a social IQ. From early childhood on children can be taught to develop social perspective and social skills. They must be provided with experiences and practice which will provide positive reinforcement for this purpose. Talk about the need for a positive self-image aside, it is important to help each child or adolescent to have repeated experiences of success in some area. This success will increase his self-esteem and his motivation for achievement. To follow up the motivation-the readiness-there must be repeated experience of success; i.e., there must be what is called a "snowball effect"-a series of successes building on each other to lead to a positive self-image in the realm of social relations which will enrich the development of the child through the contribution of friendship.

Our assumption is that positive coping successes in adolescence will be beneficial in terms of readiness and competence to cope actively and appropriately to all future life crises. Such crises often lead to isolation, loneliness and all the other negative aspects devolving from these factors. Examples of such crises could include: a crisis in marital relations, a crisis following the death of a spouse or parent, a personal crisis at work, a social or economic crisis. It is important to keep these things in mind when considering the phenomenon of a suicide by active persons, leaders in society. In each of these cases, the person attempting suicide, or those close to him, all testify that he had found himself isolated, without the support of friends, and could not cope positively with the continuing crises of his life.

It is important to add that in large secondary schools, where the emphasis is on organization, order, discipline and achievement, the condition of isolated students, who are not aggressive, may be worse because of unawareness of their problem. Loneliness is a personal perception and interpretation which turns into a confirmation of a social condition. Clinical testimony and interviews with adolescents indicate that physical presence in an active social group is not in itself enough to solve the problem of personal loneliness. It is possible, for instance, for a person who grows up in a kibbutz, which is a system where social activity is part of the ideology, to feel very lonely. It is possible for a person to remain lonely in an active youth organization in a boarding school, or for someone to be active in any number of tasks in school, at work or at home and still remain lonely. Only active experience in shaping mutual friendship-with persons of the same sex and with persons of the opposite sex-which is directed at gaining positive experience in positive intimate relationships can provide a cure for loneliness.

In the introduction of this first volume of our program for the advancement of the social development of adolescents, we have proposed a psycho-social approach and cited scientific information related to the central subjects of development of fellowship and friendship. We have closed the discussion with a look at those who fail in these social skills and find themselves lonely.

Now we shall go to Part II of this volume in which we present a variety of experiences for the use of leaders of PPS groups of adolescents for the development of social perspective and social skills.

We have defined cognitive, social and emotional tasks in three central areas of learning and behavior: Getting acquainted and the forming of the PPS Group, Developing Friendship, and Dealing with Conflicts in Friendship. The experiences were designed in accordance with our theoretical assumptions, which have been detailed in the Leader's Guide accompanying the program (Smilansky, 1990). The experiences have been tested in peer groups in various educational institutions in Israel and the United States, with attention to group composition and the personality and training of the leaders. They have been revised in accordance with feedback received in workshops held for this purpose around the country. It is our hope that each group leader will be able to select the experiences which best suit a particular group of adolescents.

BIBLIOGRAPHY

Adelson, J. and Doehrman, M.J. The psychodynamic approach to adolescence. In J. Adelson (Ed.). **Handbook of Adolescent Psychology.** New York: Wiley, 1980.

Allen, V.L. Self, social group, and social structure: Surmises about the study of children's friendships. In S.R. Asher & J.M. Gottman (Eds.). **The Development of Children's Friendships.** New York: Cambridge university Press, 1981.

Argyle, M. et al. **Social Situations.** Cambridge University Press, 1985.

Asher, S.R. & Gottman, J.M. (Eds.) **The Development of Children's Friendships.** New York: Cambridge University Press, 1981.

Asher, S.R., Oden, S.L. & Gottman, J.M. Children's friendships in school settings. In L.G. Katz (Ed.). **Current Topics in Early Childhood Education.** Norwood, NJ: Albex Co. 1977.

Asher, S.R. & Renshaw, P.D. Children without friends: Social knowledge and social-skill training. In, S.R. Asher & J.M. Gottman (Eds.). **The Development of Children's Friendships.** New York: Cambridge University Press, 1981.

Bandura, A. Social learning and the shaping of children's judgments. **Journal of Personality and Social Psychology,** 1969, 11: 275-283.

Bigelow, B.J. Children's friendship expectations: A cognitive developmental study. **Child Development**, 1977, 48: 246-253.

Bigelow, B.J. & La Gaipa, J. The development of friendship values and choice. In, H.C. Foot, A.J. Chapman & J. Smith (Eds.). **Friendship and Social Relations in Children.** New York: Wiley, 1980.

Bloss, P. **On Adolescence: A Psychoanalytic Interpretation.** New York: Free Press, 1962.

Bloss, P. **The Adolescent Passage: Developmental Issues.** New York: International Universities Press, 1979.

Bossert, S.T. **Tasks and Social Relations in Classrooms.** New York: Cambridge University Press, 1979.

Brennan, T. Loneliness in adolescence. In, L. Peplau & D. Perlman (Eds.). **Loneliness: A Source-book of Current Theory, Research and Therapy.** New York: Wiley, 1982.

Brody, G.H. A social learning explanation of moral development.

Paper presented at annual meeting of the American Educational Research Association, New York, 1977.

Bronfenbrenner, V. **The Ecology of Human Development.** Cambridge, MA: Harvard University Press, 1979.

Byrne, D. The influence of propinquity and opportunities for interaction on classroom relationships. **Human Relations,** 1961, 14: 63-69(b).

Charlesworth, R. & Hartup, W.W. Positive social reinforcement in the nursery school peer group. **Child Development,** 1967, 38: 933-1003.

Check, J., Perlman, D. & Malamut, N. Loneliness and aggressive behavior. **Journal of Social and Personal Relationships,** 1985, 2: 245-252.

Cheek, J.M. & Busch, C.M. The influence of shyness on loneliness in a new situation. **Personality and Social Psychology Bulletin,** 1981, 7: 572-577.

Cohen, E.G. Design and redesign of the desegregated school. In, W. Stephan & J. Feagin (Eds.). **School Desegregation: Past, Present and Future.** New York: Pilgrim Press, 1980(a).

Coleman, J.C. Academic achievement and the structure of competition. **Harvard Educational Review,** 1959, 29: 330-351.

Coleman, J.C. Friendships and the peer group in adolescence. In, J. Adelson (Ed.). **Handbook of Adolescent Psychology.** New York: Wiley, 1980.

Corsaro, W.A. Friendship in the nursery school: Social organization in a peer environment. In, S.R. Asher & J.N. Gottman (Eds.). **The Development of Children's Friendships.** New York: Cambridge University Press, 1981.

Duetsch, H. **The Psychology of Women.** London: Research Books, 1947.

Douvan, E. & Adelson, J. **The Adolescent Experience.** New York: Wiley, 1966.

Elkind, D. Egocentrism in adolescence. **Child Development,** 1967, 38: 1025-1034.

Epstein, J.L. & Karweit, N. (Eds.). **Friends in School.** Patterns of selection and influence in secondary schools. New York: Academic Press, 1983.

Erikson, E. **Childhood and Society.** New York: Norton, 1968.
Erikson, E. **Identity, Youth and Crisis.** New York: Norton, 1968.
Festinger, L. A theory of social comparison processes. **Human Relations,** 1954, 7: 117-140.
Flavell, J.H. **Cognitive Development.** Englewood Cliffs, NJ: Prentice Hall, 1977.
French, D. et al. Effects of cooperative, competitive and individualistic sets on performance in children's groups. **Journal of Experimental Child Psychology,** 1977, 24: 1-10.
Fromm-Reichman, F. Loneliness. **Psychiatry,** 1959, 22: 1-15.
Gottman, J.M. & Parkhurst, J.T. A developmental theory of friendship and acquaintanceship processes. In, W.A. Collins (Ed.). **Minnesota Symposia on Child Psychology,** 1980, 13.
Hallinan, M.T. Friendship patterns in open and traditional classrooms. **Sociology of Friendship,** 1976, 49: 254-264(a).
Inhelder, B. & Piaget, J. **The growth of logical thinking.** New York: Basic Books, 1958.
Ishiyama, F.J. Shyness: Anxious social sensitivity and self-isolating tendency. **Adolescence,** 1984, 19: 903-911.
Jones, W.H. et al. The persistence of loneliness: Self and other determinants. **Journal of Personality,** 1981, 49: 27-48.
Jones, W.H. Loneliness and social skills deficits. **Journal of Personality and Social Psychology,** 1982, 42: 682-692.
Kon, I.S. & Losenkov, V.A. Friendship in adolescence: Values and behavior. **Journal of Marriage and the Family,** 1978, 40: 143-155.
La Gaipa, J.A. A developmental study of the meaning of friendship in adolescence. **Journal of Adolescence,** 1979, 2: 201-213.
La Gaipa, J.A. Children's friendship In, S. Duck & R. Gilmore (Eds.) **Personal Relation 2: Developing Personal Relations.** New York: Academic Press, 1981.
Leiderman, P.M. Loneliness: A psychodynamic interpretation. **International Psychiatric Clinics,** 1969, 6: 155-174.
Lever, J. Sex differences in the games children play. **Social Problems,** 1976, 23: 478-487.
Lynch, I. **The Broken Heart: The Medical Consequences of Loneliness.** New York: Basic Books, 1977.
Maccoby, E.E. The development of moral values and behavior in

childhood. In J. Clausen (Ed.). **Socialization and Society.** Boston: Little, Brown, 1968.

Mahon, N.E. Developmental changes and loneliness during adolescence. **Topics in Clinical Nursing,** 1983, 5: 66-76.

Mannarino, A.P. The development of children's friendships. In, H.C. Foot, A.J. Chapman & J.R. Smith (Eds.). **Friendship and Social Relations in Children.** New York: Wiley, 1980.

Manor, H. Highschools' Social Climate in Israel as a Determinant of Success or Failure. Ph.D. Dissertation, Tel-Aviv University, 1981.

Offer, D. & Offer, J.B. **From Teenager to Young Manhood.** New York: Basic Books, 1975.

Parsons, T. The school class as a social system: Some of its functions in American society. **Harvard Educational Review,** 1959, 29: 297-318.

Perlman, D. & Peplau, L.A. Loneliness. In, S.W. Duck & R. Gilmore (Eds.). **Personal Relationships.** London: Academic Press, 1981.

Rubin, Z. Children without friends. In, L. Peplau & D. Perlman (Eds.). **Loneliness: A Source Book of Current Theory, Research and Therapy.** New York: Wiley, 1982.

Selman, R. **The Growth of Interpersonal Understanding: Developmental and Clinical Analyses.** New York: Academic Press, 1980.

Selman, R. The development of interpersonal competence: The role of understanding in conduct. **Developmental Review,** 1981, 1: 401-422.

Smilansky, M. **The Challenge of Adolescence on the Threshold of the 21st Century,** Information and Ideas. Gaithersburg, MD, 1990.

Spitzberg, B.H. & Cannary, D. Loneliness and relationally competent communication. **Journal of Social and Personal Relationships,** 1985, 387-402.

Spivack, G. & Shure, M. **The Social Adjustment of Young Children.** San Francisco: Jossey-Bass, 1974.

Strickland, D. Friendship patterns and altruistic behavior in preadolescent males and females. **Nursing Research,** 1981, 30: 222-235.

Sullivan, H.S. **The Interpersonal Theory of Psychiatry.** New York: Norton, 1952.

Weiss, R.S. **Loneliness: The Experience of Emotional and Social Isolation.** Cambridge, MA: MIT Press, 1973.

Williams, J.G. & Solano, C.H. The social reality of feeling lonely: Friendship and reciprocation. **Personality & Social Psychology Bulletin,** 1983, 9: 237-242.

Youniss, J. **Parents and Peers in Social Development.** Chicago: University of Chicago Press, 1980.

Zimbardo, P.G., Pilkonis, P.A. & Norwood, R.M. **The Silent Prison of Shyness.** Stanford: Stanford University Press, 1974.

Zimbardo, P.G. **Shyness.** New York: Jove: HBJ Books, 1977.

Part II: Groups Experiences

Feldman Shoshana, B.A.
Ruseman Michal, M.A.
Shelex Alina, M.A.
Smilansky Sara, Phd.
Zorman Rachel, Phd.

I. Getting Acquainted and Cohesion in Social Grpups

Introduction
The subject before us consists of activities developed for social groups (Positive Peer Support Groups — PPS) which meet on a regular basis, divided into 17 topics for experiential learning. Since the composition and needs of each group are unique, alternative exercises are suggested within each experiential area, from which the facilitator can choose the appropriate activity, according to the following principles:
* If both the group and the facilitator are new, it is best to deal with the subject completely, choosing one or two exercises from each section.
* If members of the group know each other, but the facilitator is new, it is recommended to begin with a short activity, in order to learn peoples' names (and also so that the facilitator will get to know the names of the participants right away), and with an additional exercise for a deeper introduction, a sort of "warm-up" for the group work to come.
* Even though we are dealing with the subject of consolidating the group into a single entity, it is important to remember that a group develops, coalesces, and changes during the process of working together. The facilitator must be sensitive to group dynamics, and when problems arise which affect the feeling of group solidarity or with the process of arriving at it (through working on a different subject), he must integrate appropriate exercises from t he sections on those particular subjects into the common activities.

Aims
* Understanding the concept: getting acquainted
* Learning names quickly and effectively
* Getting members of the group acquainted with each other with a minimum of self-exposure
* "Breaking the ice" and reducing the tension of the first meeting
* Developing initiative and response to initiative as a form of human interaction
* Developing readiness to meet and get acquainted with a variety of people in a variety of situations
* Getting acquainted within a social group as a social system
* Understanding the significance of the group's contribution to the individual
* Creating opportunities for mutual support within the group
* Developing readiness for mutual acceptance and exposure
* Learning mecanisms of verbal and non-berbal communication
* Learning the "rules of the game" devolving on members of the group and on the facilitator

1. Getting Acquainted for the First Time

Process
The facilitator begins: "In the framework of this group we will touch on things which are close to our hearts and which are important for getting along in life.
In order that the work we do together in the group will succeed and be of value to us, it is important to know each other really well."

Exercise A-"The Ball"
Each participant says his name. After going around the group, the facilitator takes a ball and throws it to one of the participants while saying his name. He, in turn, throws the ball to another participant, saying his name as well; this continues until all have taken part in the exercise.
One may not throw the ball twice to the same person. If the one throwing has forgotten a person's name, he can ask for a reminder and then throw it. It is a good idea to repeat the exercise at a faster pace.

Exercise B: "My Name Plus" (Alternate)
Each participant says his first name and adds a significant detail or two about himself.
At the end of the round, the participants turn their chairs around so that their backs are to the center of the circle, and write as many names as they can recall. After two-three minutes, they turn around again and find out who has recalled his name and who has forgotten.
The participants ask those whose names they forgot to repeat them.

Exercise C: "The Name-Tag" (Alternate) The facilitator has prepared colored tags, pins and markers ahead of time. At the beginning of the meeting each participant writes his name on a tag, exactly as he wishes to be called (a nickname, short form of his name, etc.), and pins it to his clothing.

Even if the participants already know each other, they should put on the name-tags so as to help the facilitator learn their names.

Participants, who are interested, can tell the group the significance of their nicknames and how they got them.

2. Deeper Acquaintance

Process:
Exercise A: "Getting Acquainted in Pairs"
1) The group is divided into couples. The couples take five minutes to introduce themselves to each other. If members of the group already know each other, they should try to tell each other something about themselves which they think the other does not know; for example, things they like or don't like, certain hobbies, their wishes, personal characteristics, etc.

   * The facilitator should introduce himself and participate as a member of the group.

2) The group is sitting around in a circle; the group members pair off, going around in order. Each participant then tells what he likes about the other. For example, "I talked with Dale, and I liked the fact that she has clear ideas about the future." or "I really liked Ted's unique point of view." etc.

   * It is important that the descriptions be specific and focused rather than general and vague; not, for example, "I like him" or "She is nice."

Exercise B: "The Same and Different" (Alternate)
1) The participants are divided into subgroups according to one of the following characteristics:
   the season in which he was born
   the month in which he was born
   his birth-order in the family (oldest, youngest, etc)

Each group tries to find two-three characteristics which are shared by the members and two-three characteristics which distinguish them from each other.
2) A representative from each group will report very briefly about the similarities and differences which were discovered in the group.

Exercise C: "The Visiting Card" (Alternate)
1) The facilitator distributes empty cards to everyone. Each participant writes four or five things, which in his opinion, characterize himself, without writing his name. For example:
   I love pop music.
   When I grow up, I want to work with computers.
   I like action films.
2) The facilitator collects all the cards, chooses one of them and reads it to the group. The group tries to identify who wrote the card.
3) Repeat the process of 2) until all the cards are read.
4) The participants discuss how they felt about the experience.

3. Readiness for and Initiating Getting Acquainted

Process:
The facilitator begins:
"Many times each one of us finds himself in situations where we have to get to know new people. For a lot of us, this is not so simple, but it is important for all of us to learn different ways to get to know others. Let's try testing different ways to get acquainted with new people in different situations."

Exercise A: "I am New Here"

1) The facilitator asks the participants to close their eyes and says very slowly:
   "You are signed up for an after-school class in your favorite hobby." (Pause)
   "You arrive on the first day, you enter the room... you feel a bit embarrassed... and you wait... The person in charge says that in order to do the first project you need to work in pairs. You don't know anyone. What do you do?" (Pause)

2) The facilitator asks the participants to open their eyes and tell what they thought about doing in such a situation.

   * The facilitator should make sure the participants begin their stories with "I..."

3) The facilitator asks the participants, who are willing, to relate their personal experiences-when they were forced to get acquainted with new people-and how they coped.

   * If the members of the group have difficulty raising personal stories, it is recommended that the facilitator bring up an example, as follows: "When I used to come to a place which was new to me, I used to sit quietly, not do a thing and I wait until someone else made the first move. Sitting like that was very hard and not very pleasant. But I didn't know how to start getting to know others, and so I just sat and waited. What do you do most of the time, when you find yourselves in the company of people you don't know?"
   * It is always better to begin with people who are willing to tell about themselves and afterwards to turn to the others. Obviously, it is not recommended to put pressure on those who still are not willing to talk.

Exercise B: "A New Place" (Alternate)
1) The facilitator distributes cards containing descriptions of different circumstances, in which one might encounter people he doesn't know, randomly to the participants. Below are some examples:
    — You are traveling alone on a bus from Washington to New York City. A girl around your age is sitting next to you....
    — You have moved to a new apartment. There are boys your age in the building. You go down to the playground and see them...
    — You go to a party with a friend. Except for him, you don't know a single person....
2) Each participant writes how he would respond in the situation described and why.
3) The facilitator reads the description of one of the circumstances and asks the participants who got that card to respond. Repeat the process for all the other circumstances.
4) The facilitator asks the participants to consider different responses, for example:
    — Is there a difference between the responses?
    — Is there a difference between boys and girls?
    — What are the reasons for the different responses? (shyness, taking initiative, avoiding initiative)
5) The facilitator asks the participants who are willing to tell about similar situations from their own experience.

* It is important to emphasize that they are getting acquainted with someone of the same sex, so that problems of sexuality can be avoided.

Exercise C: "The Delegation" (Alternate)
1) The facilitator asks two of the participants to sit in the middle of the circle, one facing the other. The facilitator says:
"Each of you has been chosen by your school to participate in a delegation to France.

* Since the aim is to examine beginning relationships, the facilitator should be sure to stop the role-play at an early stage, even before the five minutes are up.

"You do not know anyone else. You know that the person sitting next to you is a member of the same delegation. Try to strike up an acquaintance with him.
You have five minutes."
2) The facilitator asks the two participants to tell the group how they felt and what they learned about each other. After that, the two participants return to their places in the circle.
3) The facilitator choses another pair from the participants and presents them with the same situation. He requests them to try a different way to strike up an acquaintance.
4) The facilitator asks the second pair to share their feelings and what they learned about each other with the group.
5) The group as a whole relates to the different attempts to form a relationship. Participants, who are willing, tell examples from their own experience about establishing new relationships: how they felt, how hard it was, how easy it was, how they coped.

Conclusion
The facilitator begins:
"We have experienced different kinds of getting-acquainted activities. Let's try to summarize what we have learned from these experiences."
— What do you think "getting acquainted" means?
— What are the different kinds of "getting acquainted" that we are familiar with?
— What does having acquaintances give us?
— How have these experiences helped us get better acquainted with members of the group?
— Have these experiences contributed towards getting better acquainted with ourselves?
— What talents for getting acquainted have we developed?
— Could these experiences be of help in getting to know new people-outside the group-more easily?

* The participants should have the opportunity to express their opinion with regard to each point separately.

4. What is a Group?

Aim:
Awareness of the social group as a social system by means of clarification of the concepts of "group" and "social group"

Process
1) The facilitator begins:
   "We are a social group. Today we will take a look at what is the same and what is different about a social group as opposed to other groups."
   The facilitator asks the participants to tell what is a group and to describe examples of other groups that they are familiar with. The facilitator writes the examples on the board.
2) The facilitator says:
   "Scientists define a group in different ways. Let's take a look at these definitions."
   Each one receives a piece of paper with different definitions of the concept "group". The participants try to match the examples of groups to the definitions.

* It's important that there shold be a large variety of groups, such as: people watching a film, passengers in a taxi or an airplane, members of an organized tour, football team, family, (school) class.

DEFINITIONS OF THE CONCEPT "GROUP"

A group is a collection of people engaging in modes of interpersonal relationships.

A group is a collection of people engaging in mutual dependency;
anything influencing one, influences all.

A group is a social unit made up of two or more people who regard themselves as belonging to the group.

A group is a collection of people who have come together for a common purpose.

A group is a collection of people where each one of them is interested in meeting personal needs through the relationship with the group.

A group is a collection of people whose interrelationship is characterized by modes of organization and by agreed norms of behavior.

A group is a collection of people influencing each other.

3) Hold a short discussion along the following lines:
— Are there any difficulties in categorization and matching the examples?
— Which definition(s) is/are more/less appropriate?
— Can they suggest other definition(s)?

4) The facilitator concludes by saying:
"Each of the above definitions relates to a certain aspect of the concept "group" and is not a generalization. Everyone defines group according to his own needs. Defining a concept is important in order for us to have a common basis for our discussion."

He continues and asks the participants:
— How many groups can a person belong to? Give examples.
— What groups do the participants belong to?
— What sort of expectations do we have when we belong to some sort of framework; what expectations do others have with regard to us as members of that framework?

5) The facilitator divides the participants into subgroups according to the types of groups they have brought up (family, friends, class, etc.).

Each participant writes what his expectations are from the group he is a member of and what the group expects from him. For example:

"I expect that my family will support me in any circumstance."

"My family expects respect and consideration from me."

"I expect that my friends will be loyal and will help me."

"My friends expect that I will spend most of my free time with them."

6) The participants of each group will gather all the expectations in two lists:
— What are my expectations from the group?
— What are the expectations of the group from me?

A representative from each group will present the lists to the entire group.

7) To conclude, compare the expectations of the different types of groups, emphasizing the following points:
— Different individuals have similar expectations, as well as different expectations, from their membership groups.
— Different individuals understand the expectations of their group differently.
— There are gaps between the expectations of the individual in a group and the expectations of the group towards the individual.
— The stronger the feeling of belonging, the higher the expectations.
— At different points in one's life there are different expectations from the same group.

5. The Significance of the Social Group

Aim:
Awareness of the importance of the group in general and the contribution of a social group in particular.

Process:
1) The facilitator says:
   "Groups that we have been discussing are familiar frameworks. A social group is a framework that we have just experienced. When we say "social group "-what does each of us think, feel, expect about such a group?
   What are the advantages of working in such a group?"
   The participants consider the above point in a short round about which the facilitator summarizes:
   "A social group is characterized by the fact that its members are of the same age or suffer from the same problems. The uniqueness of the group is that it makes learning possible by means of life experiences in a sheltered framework. The group provides mutual support, makes it possible to see different points of view and raises different alternatives for coping with. Let's see how these advantages are realized in the following exercises."
2) The participants are divided into four groups of 4-5 each, to perform the following tasks:
   a. Group A will assemble the attached jigsaw puzzle, together as a group.

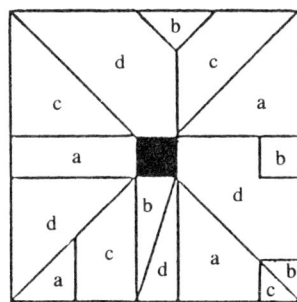

b. Each member of Group B will assemble the attached jigsaw puzzle by himself. The members of the group will sit separately, back to back.
c. Group C will make up as many words as they can from the following phrase: "THE SOCIAL GROUP". Everyone will work together with one of the group writing the words as they are said.
d. The participants of Group D will make up words as described above, but everyone will work separately, sitting back to back.

The facilitator will allow 5-10 minutes from the end of giving the instructions for this activity.

3) Compare the results of the individual activities with the group activities, especially with regard to the following points:
   a. How did each one feel while carrying out the task?
   b. How did each one feel within his group?
   c. How did the work function within the group?
   d. Were there things which interfered with the work in the group?

The discussion will conclude the meeting.

6. The Contribution of the Group in Various Coping Strategies

Aims:
* Being helped by the social group in coping with various situations.
* Awareness of the group's ability to help the individual in finding alternatives, setting priorities, budgeting time, etc.

Process:
1) The facilitator begins:
   "In our last meeting we saw how working in a group can contribute to performing a task. Today we will see how a group can help the individual cope with different situations. I am going to tell you about a certain problem and I would like to hear your suggestions.

The Problem
   Nora says:
   "A lot of things are interesting to me and I want to do all of them right now. So, I am always under pressure and never do anything! What should I do?"

   The group suggests various options.

2) The facilitator says:
   "There have been a lot of different ways to cope suggested by the people in this group. One of the problems which has been raised is the problem of organizing time and using it efficiently. This problem-which affects all of us-can work to keep us from attaining various goals. Let's find ways to make our time use more efficient."
   Each participant receives a page with a large circle drawn on it; next to the circle is the following list:
   — sleeping
   — eating, bathing, etc.
   — going to school
   — doing homework
   — seeing friends
   — reading
   — watching TV
   — playing games, hobbies, etc.
   — working: chores, jobs-either in the family or outside
   — other things

* It's possible to ask them to bring crayons or colored markers with them to the activity and then have them give each segment a different color so that the way the time is organized shows up better.

* One of the aims of this exercise is to examine one's personal understanding of how his time is budgeted; later on it is compared to the actual time organization. Therefore, they don't do any labeling at the beginning.

* It's a good idea for the facilitator to prepare his "circle of time" and use it for discussion with the entire group.

117

Each participant choses the areas which are important to him and rates them according to his priority scale. He gives each item a number, so that number one would have the highest priority. After that he divides up the "circle of time" so that it will represent the time distribution on a normal day. He can look at the list if he wishes, but he does not have to mark any area that he doesn't concern himself with. The pie-shaped areas in the circle represent the amount of time set aside, according to his understanding, for each area.

sleeping — 1/4
school — 1/4
friends, TV — just a small part, etc.

3) The participants are divided into subgroups of five members and show their circles to their companions. A short discussion takes place covering the following points:
   — Are you satisfied with how your time is organized?
   — Is there a gap between your priorities and the way your time is organized?
   — Where do you feel particularly pressured and why?
   — Where do you feel you are not investing enough effort and would like to change things?
   — Do you think it might be possible to change how you organize your time? How?

4) A representative from each group will present a summary of the discussion to the rest, emphasizing the following points:
   — Where is the greatest amount of pressure felt?
   — Suggestions for more efficient time budgeting which were agreed upon in his group.
5) The facilitator presents his own "circle of time" and tells about the conflicts he had in deciding how to budget his time and how he resolved them.

* The purpose is to emphasize that all of us have conflicts with regard to budgeting our time; using time efficiently and setting priorities can help all of us cope better.

6) The participants, who are interested, present their dilemmas in budgeting their time and the group helps them by suggesting ways to resolve them based on the summaries of the subgroup discussions and any other suggestions raised.

* It is important not to pressure any of the participants to accept or agree to any of the solutions suggested right away, but encourage them to listen to various alternatives and then decide on their own.

Conclusion
"We have seen that efficient organization of time is helpful in attaining goals. Similarly, we have seen that it is possible to get help from a social group in finding different ways to budget our time more efficiently."

7. Creating a Relaxed Atmosphere in the Group

Aims:
* Develop relaxed and close feelings between members of the group
* Develop mutual trust in the group

Process:
1) The facilitator says:
   "In order that a social group can function well, we have to create the right conditions. In our meeting

today we will try to pinpoint the significance of these conditions."

The participants are split up into couples. One partner closes his eyes and the other leads him around obstacles and in different directions. After that they change places and the first leads the second around.

2) Switch partners.

The couples stand with the back of one facing the front of the other. The second partner holds out his hands and the first lets himself fall backward, the second one catching him. Then they change places.

3) Go around the group in a short discussion covering the following points:
   — How did I feel as the one doing the leading?
   — How did I feel as the one being led?
   — How did I feel as the one falling?
   — How did I feel as the one doing the catching?

4) Hold a discussion:
   — What did we learn from the experience?
   — What does trust mean to me?
   — How do you build trust?
   — What does it mean to me when I can count on someone else?
   — What does it mean to me when they count on me? Give examples.

* The discussion should emphasize the different personal reactions and feelings. It should be made clear that it is also okay not to want to fall or be led.

The purpose is that the following points should come up in the discussion:
— trusting other people
— trusting oneself and responsibility
— creating a feeling of security for other people
— mutual trust
— the ability to ask for help from others

Conclusion

Trust is created not just because of what the group gives to the individual, but also because of what the individual is ready to give to the group. In other words there is reciprocity between the individual and the group.

8. "The Gift of Happiness"

Aim:
Trust of members of the group in giving and receiving positive reinforcement.

Process

1) The facilitator says:
   "Sometimes we forget that we can make someone else happy with little things."
   Each participant gives a "gift of happiness" to each one of the group members by writing something nice about the person on a small piece of paper.
   The writers do not sign the notes.
   The notes are written personally and specifically. Thus, not something general like: "You are nice...I like you..." but: "I like your eyes" or "I like to hear your opinions" or "You have interesting ideas" etc.
   No one is to be skipped. Even if it is hard, something nice must be found about each one.

2) Each participant receives the notes meant for him (or the piece of paper folded like a fan), looks at what is written and tells the group one of the following things: what he felt when he got his "gifts"; what he learned about himself; if they met his expectations; anything new he discovered because of them; any changes in his opinion about himself; etc.

3) The facilitator asks the participants to tell how they felt as someone giving the gifts. Was it difficult? If so, in what way? How did they overcome the difficulties? What did they learn from the responses of those getting the gifts?

* The facilitator places envelopes on the table: one for each person in the group; each envelope has the name of a participant written on it.

* Each participant will get a number of notes equal to the number of participants in the group. The participants will head the note: "a gift of happiness" and will place the notes in the correct envelopes.

* The facilitator should see to it that the participants relate to their "gifts" in a general fashion and not describe exactly what was written, so as not to embarrass someone who has not received such complimentary "gifts."

9. Constructive Criticism

Aim:

Trust in giving and receiving constructive criticism.

Process:

1) The facilitator says:

    "In our last meeting we saw how nice it was to get positive reinforcement. Sometimes we find ourselves in situations where we would like to cause a change in someone's behavior without hurting anyone's sensibilities. Let's try a few exercises in this direction."

    The participants are divided into three groups. Each group receives a description of one of the circumstances described below and acts out responses using role-play. If any members of a group seem interested, they may bring up situations from their own experience and try to act them out in the group.

Circumstances:

The Shy Person
Sherry almost never opens her mouth. When she does say something she always whispers... even important things, things which are relevant and contribute to the discussion. How can we help her?

Dreaming Beauty
My best friend is sure she is the best looking and sexiest girl around and that all the guys are just "dying" to meet her. But I know that the guys don't feel that way at all. As her best friend I have tried to wake her up, but she always changes the subject. How can I help her?

The King of the Crowd
Your good friend always has something to say about everything. Not only that, but he says it loudly! He is sure that everyone thinks he really knows what he is talking about. You find his behavior bothersome and embarrassing. How can you help him?

2) Each group acts out their sociodrama before the entire group. The others suggest alternatives by getting involved in the roles being enacted.

* After each role-play it is important to ask the participants how they felt when they received the constructive criticism and how they felt as givers of constructive criticism.

3) Go around the group, asking for examples of effective criticism that the participants have experienced.

* The facilitator could enumerate a few examples of effective criticism:
— Don't make generalizations, but talk about specific behavior: for example, if someone starts yelling, don't say: "You are always yelling; you are so dumb; you have no manners" rather say: "You are raising your voice. Now you are yelling."
— Reflect his feelings back to him: "I understand that you are angry." "I understand from what you are saying that you feel humiliated."
— Say what happens to you as a result of his behavior: "It is hard for me to answer you when you yell." "I really feel good when you listen to me and pay attention to what I say."

— Express your perception of the other person: "It seems to me that you are angry at me. Is that right?" "It seems to me that you are giving in about your rights awfully easily." "I get the feeling that you aren't terribly interested when others are talking."

4) Organize an additional short round discussing the question: How can we know when constructive criticism will be effective?

* Criticism is effective when the recipient can accept it, relate to it and do something about it.
* Effective criticism causes a change in feelings, in perception or in behavior.

This round will conclude the exercise.

10. Asking the Group for Help

Aim:
Becoming aware of what sort of help you can get from the group.

Process:
1) The facilitator says:
   "We have seen that a group can help the individual cope with lots of difficulties by suggesting different options. What else can a group do to help?"

   * This means physical aid, emotional support, etc.

2) The facilitator says:
   "Let's try to see what group help really means by looking at these circumstances."

The facilitator reads "The New Crowd" to the group and asks the participants to tell how each one of them could help the young girl. After that, the facilitator could read another short piece, "Easily Embarrassed", and once again asks the group to figure out how they could help.

Circumstances:

The New Crowd

"In a new crowd where I don't know a soul, I don't dare open my mouth. People think I can't talk! Like I'm a mute or something. When they invite me to parties, I say no, and it seems to me that I am losing touch with people and in a little while I won't have any friends."

— How can someone overcome shyness?

Easily Embarrassed

"I get embarrassed by everything! It seems like my natural color is brick red! Even my best friend manages to make me blush and want to crawl under the floor."

— How can he change his behavior?

3) The facilitator says:

"We have been discussing imaginary circumstances. Now let's think about something that each one of us would like to get help with from our friends in the group."

The facilitator asks one of the participants, who is willing, to stand at one side of the room. The rest of the participants stand in a line opposite him on the other side of the room. The volunteer presents the problem he wants help with to the other group members.

* Only people who really want to need to suggest help or solutions.
* Members should try not to repeat suggestions that have already been made.

One of the group suggests something. If the volunteer feels that the suggestion has any merit, the person suggesting it moves forward a few steps. Then someone else makes another suggestion, and the volunteer considers it and moves him forward according to his feelings about the solution. If the suggestion is too general or simple, the volunteer could tell him to move forward only one step. The more appropriate the solution suggested, the more steps forward the person will move. The volunteer will thank each person personally for making a suggestion and his expression of thanks will reflect his feelings towards the suggestion itself. For example:

"Thanks, I will think about it."

"Thanks, you have helped me a lot."

"Thanks, I will really think about it."

After 3-4 suggestions the facilitator will ask for another volunteer. It is possible to repeat the process several times.

4) The facilitator asks the "volunteers" to share their feelings with the group, both as regards their asking for help and as regards the suggestions that they got.

Afterwards the facilitator asks other members of the group to express their feelings about the procedure.

5) To conclude, the facilitator holds a brief round of discussion in which the group describes what they have gotten out of the exercise.

11. Developing Communications Skills

Aims:
* Illustrating problems in listening
* Developing discussion skills

Process:
1) The facilitator says:
   "In our previous meetings we dealt with openness in the group, mutual support, expressing trust and getting reinforcement. In order to be able to accomplish all these things well, we need to develop skills in communicating."
   The facilitator asks two participants to talk to each other in front of the whole group about any subject they want. When A speaks, B indicates in any way that he thinks is clear that he is not listening. Then, they switch roles. B speaks and A shows that he is not listening. At the end of the activity each participant is asked to tell about what he felt in other, similar situations.

   * It is suggested to distribute pieces of paper before the activity with subjects written on them or a few interjectory remarks meant to be used in the interruptions. These can be:
     — If we're already talking about this, well....
     — That reminds me, ...
     — It's good that you mentioned that because...
     — Do you remember when...
     — That's just like...
     — That's nothing, let me tell you ...

2) The facilitator asks 5-6 participants to sit in the middle of the circle.
   1. One participant begins to tell about something exciting or interesting that happened to him. Each of the other participants can interrupt the story and make him talk about something else: recalling something similar that happened to them, change the subject altogether, etc.
   The participants can interrupt also the ones who are interrupting and thus change the story a lot of times. The subject of the story will be different at the end than what it was at the beginning.

   * The facilitator will determine that the group has understood the instructions and has begun the discussion before the volunteer returns.

127

2. After five minutes of this "conversation" the facilitator stops it and asks the participants about their feelings, about the difficulties in listening or in speaking when no one is listening.
3. Afterwards the facilitator asks those who were watching to express their feelings and opinions about the "conversation."

Alternate Activities
1) The facilitator asks three volunteers to leave the room. The rest of the participants are divided into three groups. Each group receives an "instruction card" which explains how they are to behave when the volunteer who is outside returns and joins them. The card is hidden and is only known to the members of the group that received it.

INSTRUCTION CARD NO. 1
"You are to accept the newcomer and help him take part in the discussion."

INSTRUCTION CARD NO. 2
"You are to continue your discussion and ignore the newcomer's attempts to join in the discussion."

INSTRUCTION CARD NO. 3
"A newcomer is about to join your group, you may allow him to join in the discussion or not, according to how you feel."

2) Each group chooses a discussion topic and begins to talk.
3) The facilitator requests that the three volunteers come back into the room and tells each of them to join one of the groups and take part in the discussion.

* It's possible to appoint an observer for each group whose job will be to watch the behavior of the participants.

4) After about five minutes the facilitator stops the activity and asks the participants to return to the group as a whole. The volunteers tell, each in turn, how the members of the group related toward them, if they succeeded in joining in the discussion, what they felt, etc. The facilitator asks the other participants to relate to the process of the activity. The observers can also add their reports and impressions.

12. Attention to Verbal and Non-Verbal Communication

Aims:
* Awareness of verbal and non-verbal expressions of paying attention
* Awareness of the importance of matching verbal and non-verbal messages, and its influence on paying attention and making associations

1) The facilitator asks the participants to relate to the following point: "Sometimes we say: I hear you and sometimes I am listening to you. What is the difference between the two situations? Let's take a look at some examples of each."

2) The facilitator asks a couple of the participants to have a conversation in front of the entire group on any subject they wish. When A speaks, B listens. At the end of the talking, he must repeat what was said in his own words. Afterwards, they change roles: B talks and A listens, repeating what B said in his own words.
At the end of the exercise each participant will tell how he felt in each situation.

* The participants can choose one of the following subjects or one of their own:
— the importance of homework
— the significance of youth groups like scouts, campfire girls, etc.
— capital punishment as a deterrent
— allowances
— working part-time during vacations

— laws to limit the content of television programs-violence, sex, commercialism

Alternate for Exercise 2)
The facilitator invites three participants to take part in the discussion as "A" "B" and "C".
Each participant gets a sheet with discussion topics written on it or he may choose a topic he wishes to use.
A speaks first;
B listens first;
C comments first.
A speaks for two minutes,
B must summarize in his own words what A says without writing anything down. A and B may correct any errors in B's summary.
C is responsible to make sure that B doesn't distort, interpret, add to, leave out, etc. He is also responsible to observe the non verbal behavior of the other two.
The facilitator asks each of the three to relate to the following
points:
> How did each of you feel about your role?
> What were the difficulties you had with your roles? (as a spokesperson, listener, commentator).

The facilitator allows the observers to comment on the discussion.

A short discussion ensues within the entire group about the following points:
— Why is it important that verbal and non-verbal messages be the same?
— How is it possible to express attention non-verbally?
— How do we prefer others to listen to us?
— Does the amount of attention paid by other people and the way they pay attention to us affect our own readiness to listen to them?

* nodding agreement, making intermediate evaluations, facial expressions, eye contact, body gestures, repeating certain words which are spoken like "I understand from what you say that..."

— How is it possible to improve our ability to listen?
— How is it possible to make sure others will listen to us?

The discussion concludes the exercise.

13. Expressing Emotion

Aim:
Help in understanding the process of expressing emotions, both verbally and non-verbally.

Process:
1) The facilitator says:
   "Until now we have been dealing with listening skills. Now we will deal with expressing feelings both verbally and non verbally."

   The facilitator chooses two of the participants and asks them to come to the center of the circle and demonstrate the non-verbal expression of feelings in front of the group.

   The facilitator will give the pair a list of feelings, like: anger, fondness, embarrassment, sadness, excitement, etc. and they must pick one of the emotions.

   After the demonstration-the group guesses which feeling it was. This process is repeated for two or three other feelings with the emphasis on the non-verbal expression.

Additional Alternate Exercise

   The participants are divided into groups and each group is asked to draw different emotions: sadness, happiness, dread, fear, anger, etc.

   Each group presents its drawings and notes the similarities and differences from one expression to another.

2) The facilitator chooses two participants and asks them to express a double message: that is to express one message verbally and the opposite non-verbally. For example, to say "I appreciate you" in a careless tone of voice, or "I care about you" while turning one's back on you or while avoiding eye contact, etc. This process can be repeated by two or three participants.
3) Have a short discussion about the following points:
   — What do you feel about the two kind of messages-where one thing is expressed verbally and something else non-verbally?
   — Which kind is more important?
   — Is it important to make sure that the verbal and non-verbal messages are the same?
   — What feelings are connected with eye contact?

The discussion concludes the exercise.

14. Communication and Cooperation

Aim:
Improving cooperation and non-verbal modes of communication

Process:
1) The facilitator says:
   "In order to make the significance of non-verbal communication more real, let's try this exercise:
   We have to rearrange the room so that we are sitting in a giant U shape. You may not speak or move furniture around to show what must be done. You have two minutes."
   The participants report how successful they were in completing the task. How did they feel? How did they manage to communicate with their friends?

2) The participants are paired off. Each couple gets a pencil and a piece of paper which is divided into four sections. As a unit, holding the pencil together and without speaking, the couple must draw the following items: a house in the first section, a tree in the second. Then one of the partners moves on to the next pair and once again, as a unit and without speaking, the new couple draws a boy or girl in the third section and anything they like in the fourth section. Afterwards they present the drawings to the entire group and describe:
   — the work process with different partners
   — the amount of agreement between the partners
   — the degree of reciprocal expectations
   — the cooperation and amount of satisfaction
3) Hold a concluding discussion during which the significance of communication in cooperative activity is emphasized.

15. Speaking and Listening

Aim:
Development of reciprocity among the members of the group as "speakers" and "listeners"

Process:
1) The facilitator says:
   "We have been dealing with skills of group discussion and communication, with the assumption that whatever is being said in the group is interesting and significant to everybody. Things being discussed in the group don't always interest everyone or benefit everyone to the same degree. Let's talk about this a bit.
   Please close your eyes and settle comfortably into your chairs.

Everybody think about a circumstance when you are sitting with a group of friends and it is really boring. You feel like everything is sort of far off,
— what do each of you feel?
— what did each of you want to do?
— what did each of you actually do?"

* In order to create the mood of a "directed fantasy" the facilitator should speak slowly, with long pauses, in a quiet, relaxed voice.

2) The participants open their eyes and share their feelings and reactions with their friends.
A brief discussion is held according to the following points:
— What do I do when someone tells me something boring?
— How do I, when I am the one talking, know if others want to listen to me or not?
— How can I feel better about those who are listening to me?
— How can I make myself a better "speaker" so that people will want to listen to me?

* The aim is to arrive at the idea that listener-response is dependent on the quality of the interrelationship between the speaker and the listener.
* The group can suggests different options for coping with similar situations.
* The points raised should include choosing interesting subjects, fluency, diction, brevity, making eye-contact, proper posture, smiling, etc.

3) The facilitator says:
"People are different from each other in how they regard speaking. There are those who like to speak more and those who like to speak less. Let's all think how we would define ourselves: a speaker or a non-speaker?"
Go around the group with each person saying how he would define himself. Now, the facilitator asks everyone to get up and gathers all the "speakers" on one side of the room and all the "non-speakers" on the other side.

4) The "speakers" form a circle with the "non-speakers" sitting around them as observers. The facilitator asks the "speakers" to discuss a certain subject that he determines.
The discussion lasts between 5-10 minutes.

* The observation can be organized according to the number of people in each group: an observer for every speaker, an observer for every two speakers, etc.

5) Now, change places with the "non-speakers" in the middle and the "speakers" as observers.
Once again the facilitator gives out a topic for discussion, but this time he makes certain it is an exciting subject. The facilitator stops the discussion after about 10 minutes.

6) The participants return to their places in the group as a whole. The facilitator asks each one to tell how he felt and what he learned about himself. The report should be made in the following order: "speakers", observers of the "speakers", "non-speakers" and finally the observers of the "non-speakers."

7) A concluding discussion is held according to the following points:
— What did everyone get out of the exercise?
— In which situations did each one feel most comfortable?
— In which situations did each one feel uncomfortable?
— How could this be applied to future behavior?

16. Work-Style in a Social Group

Aims:
* Increasing cooperation despite competitiveness
* Learning the "rules of the game" in a social group
* Examining the amount of cohesion in a social group

Process:
1) The participants are divided into groups of 4-5 members each. Each group gets a bottle with 4-5 tokens (coins with a hole in the middle) or beads inside, each having a string attached.

    Each participant must get his token or bead out of the bottle as quickly as possible by pulling its string.

    The first participant in each group to pull his token or bead out of the bottle gets 20 points.

    The first group which succeeds in emptying its bottle gets 10 points per member.

    * The bottle needs to have a neck narrow enough so that only one token or bead may be pulled through at a time.
    * The idea is that in order to succeed the group members need to take turns pulling out their tokens/beads.
    * The point is giving up one's personal benefit for the good of the group.

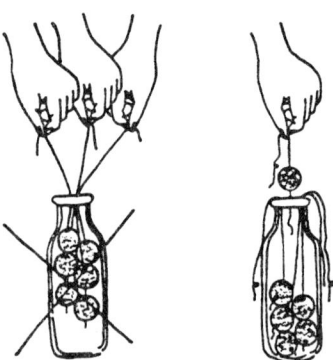

2) Hold a round of discussion in which they relate to these questions:
    — What did everyone feel?
    — What can you learn from the activity?

3) Hold an additional round of discussion about this question:
   — What can be done in order to improve the work-style of the group?

   * The facilitator should direct the discussion so that someone brings up the need to set out "rules of the game" which are obligatory on everybody. That is to say, a "social contract" covering acceptable behavior between members of the group.

4) At the end of the discussion the participants are divided into four groups. Each group suggests ideas and subjects which could be part of a constitution. The point is to become aware not of the content of the activity but of the process of accomplishing it.

   * The facilitator should circulate around the groups. If he finds that they are not bringing up constructive ideas, he can suggest examples like a logo or flag, a group name, officers, parliamentary procedure, etc.

5) A representative from each sub-group presents the ideas that came up to the whole group. The entire group discusses them and arrives at an agreement about various of the ideas.

6) The participants are divided into groups according to the topics that they agreed upon, and each group, according to its choice, focuses on putting the idea into effect. For example: drawing up a logo or designing a flag, drawing up rules of behavior, determining obligatory attendance, deciding on the type of meeting (with or without refreshments), etc.

7) Each group presents what it has done before the entire group. After evaluations and clarifications from each of the groups, a group constitution is drawn up which is obligatory on everyone. Two members volunteer to write it up in a nice format: a scroll, a newsletter, a booklet, etc.

17. Evaluation of work style

An Alternate Exercise to Paragraphs 3-7

3) The facilitator says:
"We have participated in various activities whose purpose was to improve the style of working within the group. Let's see how every one of you feels about the group."

Each participant fills out the following questionnaire:

How I feel about the Group

When you are in a social group, to what degree, in your opinion, do you feel comfortable about doing the following things. Please circle the number which represents your reaction to each sentence: 1 = I feel very uncomfortable, 2 = I feel pretty uncomfortable, 3 = I feel pretty comfortable, 4 = I feel very comfortable.

		I feel very uncomfortable	I feel pretty uncomfortable	I feel pretty comfortable	I feel very comfortable
1.	Say I am glad to meet someone	1	2	3	4
2.	Agree with the opinions and feelings of one of the group members	1	2	3	4
3.	Encourage one of the group members to finish telling about an idea of his	1	2	3	4
4.	Ask one of the group members to explain what he just said	1	2	3	4
5.	Ask one of the group members to say what he thinks about different things	1	2	3	4

		I feel very uncomfortable	I feel pretty uncomfortable	I feel pretty comfortable	I feel very comfortable
6.	Ask one of the group members to talk about himself	1	2	3	4
7.	Suggest things to the group	1	2	3	4
8.	Express my personal opinion	1	2	3	4
9.	Summarize what someone else in the group has said	1	2	3	4
10.	Say that I disagree with something someone in the group has said	1	2	3	4
11.	Express justified criticism of someone in the group	1	2	3	4
12.	Disagree with the facilitator	1	2	3	4
13.	Talk about my feelings in front of the group	1	2	3	4
14.	Share a personal experience with the group	1	2	3	4

After the group finishes filling out the questionnaire, the facilitator asks them to look at the questionnaire and comment on those things that they indicated they were comfortable with in the group. The discussion should focus on these points:
— What are the similarities between the participants in terms of what makes them feel comfortable?
— Are there significant differences?
— Do they remember how they felt about those things when the group first began to meet?

— Can they give examples of how the group has developed?
— About what points do people still feel uncomfortable?
— How can these things be improved?

Evaluation

If the facilitator feels it is necessary, he can ask the participants to illustrate the feeling of group cohesion in some way (group drawing, play, graph).

II. Friendship

1. Introduction

The main goal of the exercises suggested from here on is to strengthen the ability of the individual to enter into and carry on friendship relationships at various levels and in accordance with different needs.

Dealing with this subject will help the individual to become acquainted with himself, to know his own positive and negative features, both as a friend and a person. Similarly, it can strengthen his awareness and sensitivity to other people's need for reciprocity, implicit in all human relations.

The ability to enter into and carry on friendship relationships will help the individual in forming relationships in various types of frameworks including the family and workplace.

Experiential work in social groups helps by raising problems and displaying various options for resolving them. In order to bring the participants closer to the topic, to encourage openness in the group and to make it easier to bring up personal problems, it is recommended to begin with general subjects and to approach more significant and personal matters only gradually. However, if the facilitator feels that the group is ripe for discussing personal matters, it is possible to skip over the beginning stage and enable the participants to bring up personal experiences and situations. Notwithstanding all the foregoing, it is of utmost importance that the facilitator should be sensitive to group process and to the degree of exposure which is appropriate.

An additional goal in group work is developing sensitivity to all the implications of a subject under discussion, to be able to delve deeply into it and to improve the ability to apply lessons learned to behavior in various realms.

The subjects are chosen according to a certain developmental approach and therefore it is advised to maintain the order presented here.

Aims:
* Understanding the concept of friendship and its significance at different ages (satisfaction of different needs, expression of similarities and differences between human beings, etc.)
* Awareness of the conditions necessary for establishing friendly relations (mutual obligation, tolerance for self-exposure, ability to give and receive emotional, verbal support, tolerance for change)
* Understanding the conditions necessary for establishing friendship
* Learning ways to cope with confrontation in friendship
* Recognition of different modes of friendship for girls and for boys
* Learning ways of ending friendship ties
* Awareness of the problem of loneliness
* Making new friends
* Accepting the "different" in the friendship group

1. What is "friendship"?

Aim:
To understand the concept of friendship and its significance at different ages.

Process:
1) A short discussion is held in which the participants make associations with the word "friendship".
   The facilitator writes down the main words brought up on the board.

2) The facilitator says:
"We have seen that the concept of 'friendship' has many meanings. Let's see if these meanings change as we go along in life." The participants are divided into four groups where each group is made up of all members of the same sex (two groups of boys and two groups of girls). Each group discusses the meaning of "friendship" at the age of childhood and at the age of the participants and keeps track of the things brought up.

* The facilitator emphasizes that what is being discussed is real friendship and not simply acquaintanceship.
* It is possible to relate to the meaning of friendship for older people as well, for example: for parents.

3) Each group presents its list and holds a short discussion according to the following points:

— What characterizes friendship at the age of childhood?

* Point out sharing activities, living close by, etc. the result of a small amount of mutual obligation.
* Point out looking for similarities by accepting differences, greater mutual obligation, filling each others needs, consideration and giving emotional support, helping people cope with their problems.

— What characterizes friendship at the age of youth?

— What characterizes friendship at an older age?
— What is the difference between girls and boys with regard to these points?

* It is reasonable to assume that the question of friendship between the sexes will arise. The facilitator will say that at this stage we will only deal with friendship between people of the same sex and will discuss friendship between members of the opposite sex later on.

4) The facilitator keeps the lists and a summary of the discussion (which he writes down) for the next meeting and says:
"Let's see if the characteristics for each age that the groups have brought up match reality. In order to do this, let's break up into couples. Each couple will interview:
   —a child (boy or girl)
   —a teenager (boy or girl)
   —an adult (man or woman)
and will ask each of them:
   In your opinion, what is a good friend?
Bring the answers in writing to the next meeting."

2. Friendship at different ages

Aim:
Ascertaining the meaning of friendship at different ages-a field test

Process:
1) The facilitator asks the participants to tell, in a brief round of discussion, about their experiences and feelings during the interview.
2) The participants are divided into groups which consist of three interviewer-couples each.
   Each group reviews the interviews and writes down the results on a page containing the following table:

Age of Interviewee	Couple A	Couple B	Couple C
Child	m/f	m/f	m/f
Teenager	m/f	m/f	m/f
Adult	m/f	m/f	m/f
General Comments:			

3) Each group presents its notes to the entire group which will then relate to the findings of the various groups by comparing what was noted to what had been summarized during the previous meeting.
4) The facilitator says:
"We have seen that there is a difference in what friendship means according to age and sex. In the next meeting we will try to find out other meanings of "friendship."

3. Criteria for Choosing a Friend

Aim:
Becoming acquainted with different bases for establishing friendship, such as having similar or different personal characteristics, sharing interests, filling different needs.

Process:
1) The facilitator says:
"Imagine that you have to spend a whole month on a deserted isle. You need not worry about your basic needs (food, clothing, shelter). You may choose one person (of the same sex) to be with you for the entire month on the island. Consider the following details as you decide whom you would take with you:
— age
— physical appearance
— two character traits you consider most important for him to have
— two character traits you consider most important for him NOT to have."
2) Several of the participants tell about the characteristics they would choose for someone whom they would take with them to the island and the

* In order to make the idea more concrete, you can describe different circumstances, different needs, different characteristics-for example you could describe in addition to (or instead of) the deserted isle-the following activity:
1. Each participant considers one of his friends, of the same sex, that he might pick to work on some task together (like a history project) and writes two important aspects of his character that recommended him as

reasons they chose them. The participants who wish tell how they are similar or different from the person they would take to the island.

Hold a brief discussion about the difficulties they expect the two people to have in their life together on the island, the advantages and disadvantages to a friendship between two people who have a lot in common as opposed to a friendship between two people who are different from each other. The discussion concludes the meeting.

a choice. Afterwards, he considers another friend, also of the same sex, that he would choose to go to a party with and writes two important aspects of his character like for the other one.

2. Compare the results of various situations, while emphasizing the reasons for making the choices and the characteristics which are appropriate for each situation.

4. Characteristics of a Friend and Their Contribution within the Friendship Process

Aim:
An awareness of how the various characteristics of friends contribute to the friendship process

Process:
1) The facilitator says:
   "Everyone of us needs to establish ties with people who fill different functions for us, like parents, teachers, friends. Let's us all think about activities and different situations in which we can be helped by friends or things that are nice to do with friends and write them down. For example: going to a movie, getting advice, preparing schoolwork."

* It is also important to emphasize points like expressing feelings (happiness, sadness, anger, pain, etc.), sharing experiences (finding relief); feeling secure as a result of being "together".

2) The participants read their lists. The facilitator picks 8-10 activities or situations from the lists which appeared most frequently and writes them on the board.
3) Each participant copies the situations which he had chosen, thinks about his own friends (not necessarily from the group) and writes who he would chose to do each of the activities with or be with in the situations.
4) The facilitator says: "Let's take a look at the things which you chose. What can each of us learn from this?"
5) Hold a brief discussion about the following points:
   — Did most of the participants chose one friend for most of the situations or did they chose one friend per activity?
   — Is it possible, or even desirable, that one friend meet many needs?
   — Is it preferable to search for a "perfect" friend who will fulfill different needs or to search for different friends for different purposes?
   — Is there a difference between boys and girls in their search for a single friend rather than many friends?
6) The facilitator says:
   "We have seen that we chose friends according to how similar or different we are, depending on what our needs and goals are. Now let's see in what way our characteristics and those of our friends contribute to the friendship process."
   Each participant thinks about one of his close friends and tries to pick out two "good" characteristics which are typical of this friend and how each one of these characteristics is expressed and contributes to the friendship between them.
   The facilitator gives the group 2-3 minutes of silence in which to think.

* It is a good idea that after an explanation the facilitator describe an example from his personal experience. For example, "Two characteristics which my good friend has are adventurousness and light-heartedness. These characteristics mean that he always has exciting ideas and he is always in

7) One of the participants begins to tell the group about his friend and how what he's like contributes to the friendship. The facilitator asks another participant to tell about different characteristics or about the same ones but which have a different effect on the friendship.

The facilitator summarizes briefly and says: "We have seen that different characteristics of our friends contribute in varied ways to the friendship process. In the next meeting let's try to examine how our characteristics contribute to the friendship process."

a good mood. Therefore, it is very nice to be with him, I find him interesting and forget my problems when I am with him."

5. Personal Characteristics and their Contribution to the Friendship Process

Aims:
* Awareness that our personal characteristics permeate the entire friendship process
* Developing the ability to make discoveries about our own personal characteristics from the friendship process
* Awareness of characteristics which damage the friendship process

Process:
1) The facilitator says:
"In our last meeting we related to our friends' characteristics. Today let's deal with our own characteristics and how they contribute to friendship. Each of us should think about two of our own good characteristics and how they contribute

* The facilitator announces the time limit (five minutes) at the start of the exercise in order to allow the participants to budget their time properly.

148

to the relations between ourselves and our friends."
The participants break up into pairs, according to where they are sitting, and tell each other about what they have thought of.
2) Without indicating his name, each one writes down one or two good qualities which he feels don't get expressed in his behavior but which he would like to express in his relationships with his friends. He folds the piece of paper.
3) The facilitator collects the folded pieces papers in a basket or other container, and asks one of the participants to pick a piece of paper from the basket, read the quality or qualities written on the paper and suggest a good way to express this quality in a friendship. The rest of the members of the group may add alternative suggestions. Repeat the process.
4) The facilitator asks the participants to bring up one or two qualities which bother them most in the friendship process. The facilitator writes the qualities which are raised on the board.
5) A pair of participants chooses one of the qualities written on the board and role-plays how the quality affects behavior. In other words, one of the partners acts in a way appropriate to that quality and the other partner reacts.

For example, a braggart-one of the participants acts like a braggart coming to a party and the other as a friend who is already at the party.

After the role-play each of the two players tells what he felt while playing the role and what he learned. The other participants express their opinions about the interaction and its implications rather than about the actual situation. The other participants can act out the same characteristic(s) in different ways.

This process can be repeated for several additional characteristics.

6) Hold a brief, concluding discussion around the following points:
    — a disliked quality-does it annoy the other participants and to the same degree? Or, does it bother me if I have it or does it bother me if other people have it? To what degree in either of the situations?
    — a disliked quality-does it annoy to the same degree in different situations? With different people? It's a good idea to use concrete examples.
    — Is it important to try to change disliked qualities, or should we simply accept them as a natural part of life and learn to live with them?

6. Qualities and Behavior which Damage the Friendship Process

Aim:
Presenting different ways of changing qualities and behavior which obstruct friendship

Process:
1) The facilitator says:
   "Let's see how it is possible to help the individual change qualities which bother him."
   The participants are divided into four groups of the same sex: two groups of boys and two groups of girls.
   Each group gets a letter which has been written to a newspaper writer of an advice column for youth. They must suggest various possibilities for coping and producing change.

* The facilitator should prepare the letters printed here on pieces of paper to be handed out at the time of the exercise.

EXAMPLES OF LETTERS TO "YOUTH ADVICE" COLUMN

"Blowing My Top"

Anytime I take part in a conversation I burst out and want to have the last word. It is difficult for me to control myself and listen to others patiently. As a result everyone gets mad at me and I end up in a fight. What should I do?

"Blocked and Locked Up"

I want to tell my friends about problems which really bother me, but I get embarrassed and am afraid they'll make fun of me. What should I do?

2) Each group presents the problem and suggested solutions to the whole group.
The other participants can add solutions.
3) Compare the solutions which are suggested by boys and those suggested by girls. The participants should relate to similarities and differences, to reasons and signification.
4) Those participants who are prepared and interested can bring up personal qualities and ask the group to relate to different possible ways of coping with them.

Conclusion We have seen that personality characteristics permeate the entire friendship process. But we don't always present all the sides of our personality the way we would like people to see them. We have learned how to identify additional qualities of ourselves in the friendship process. Similarly, we have seen how it is possible to change qualities or behavior which bother us in the friendship process.

7. The Expectations Gap between Friends

Aims:
* Understanding the reasons for "lows" in friendship
* Examination of the possible "ways out" of low periods or situations producing lows which occur among friends

Process:
1) The facilitator says:
   "One of the reasons for 'downs' in friendships is the 'expectations gap' between friends. Let's try to illustrate this."

   The participants are divided into four groups. Each group receives a discussion topic which involves the description of a circumstance which it must transform into a telephone conversation, a face-to-face dialogue, or a role-play which would demonstrate the expectations gap and which would raise the possibilities of dealing with such a gap.

DISCUSSION TOPICS (Descriptions of Circumstances)

1.	I love it most when I spend a lot of time with my friend and he shares all his troubles with me. My friend is satisfied to see me just once a week.
2.	I want to be friends, heart and soul, and she just wants to go to the movies and parties with me.
3.	Joey wants a relationship like in the drawing below: 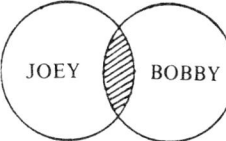 However, Bobby wants a relationship which is like this drawing: 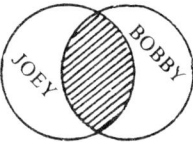 What will happen to this friendship?

4. Amy wants an exclusive friendship with me, and I am interested in keeping my ties with Katie and Alice.

2) Each group presents the dialogues or role-plays to the entire group.

* It is possible to exchange roles where the participant who presents the problem plays the role of the friend (in order to give the individual the chance to experience his friend's point of view.

153

3) The facilitator asks one of the participants, who is willing, to present a personal problem of an expectations gap and to ask the group to help him deal with this gap. The group suggests different ways of dealing with the gap which has been revealed.

* The end of a friendship is also a legitimate solution- when there is no possibility to bridge the gap.

Conclusion
We have seen that everyone has different expectations from his friends. Sometimes there is no gap between the expectations between those sharing a friendship and sometimes there is. It is possible to deal with these gaps in various ways.

8. Conflicts within Friendship

Aims:
* Becoming acquainted with different conflicts within friendship, like revealing secrets, gossip, jealousy, etc.
* Dealing with these conflicts using different types of responses

To the Facilitator:
These next meetings deal with different conflicts which arise in friendship situations and the ways in which to respond to them. There are alternate exercises suggested below. In order that each group can deal with the conflicts which bother them the most, the first activity suggested is one of identification and rating the conflicts. The facilitator can choose the appropriate exercises according the ratings made within the groups.

Process:
1) The facilitator says;
    "In the earlier meetings we saw there is a high point in friendship, an overlapping of the expectations of the friends. The extent of the high points and overlapping depends on good feelings and satisfaction within the friendship process. We have seen, despite this, that there are also low points and gaps in expectations. The low points are the result of various conflicts. Clashes and quarrels between friends which arise from different sources and the importance of which changes from person to person.
    Let's see what are the main reasons for such things in our own group."
    Each participant fills out the paper titled "Conflicts between Friends" (below)

Conflicts between Friends

This is a list of topics that could cause clashes between friends. Make an "x" in the appropriate place in order to indicate to what degree each topic bothers you.

Conflict	Bothers Me A Lot	Bothers Me Medium	Bothers Me A Little
Tale-bearing (tattling)			
Gossip			
Disloyalty			
Telling secrets			
(Over) sensitivity			
Insults			
Wanting to make friends with a third person			
Competitiveness			
Jealousy			

2) The facilitator writes the topics causing clashes on the board and indicates how many times each was indicated as a very annoying issue.

Gossip
1) Each participant completes the following sentence appropriately (boys gossip about boys, girls about girls):

   * Since we are dealing with sensitive subjects, if there are people in the group whose names are being used as the "examples", change the names in the examples.

   Aaron is gossiping with Jack and says:
   _____

   Nancy is gossiping with Ellen and says:
   _____

2) Boys should read their answers only to other boys; girls should read their answers only to other girls. The facilitator sorts the answers by sex and records them in two columns on the board.
3) The participants are divided into 3-4 mixed groups (boys and girls together) and discuss the following questions:
   1. We have seen that everyone understands the idea of gossip in a different way. Is it possible to arrive at one or maybe more definitions of "gossip"?
   2. According to the lists on the board is there any difference between the way boys and girls understand the idea of "gossip"? What is that difference?

   * The survey and conversation of the entire group will occur after the discussion of the two questions. There is no need to press for a single definition which the whole group agrees with.

4) A representative from each group reports to the group as a whole about the conclusions that were arrived at within his subgroup for the second question—the differences between boys and girls, and after that he reports about the different understandings of the idea of gossip.

5) The facilitator prepares six pieces of paper which contain information about a boy named Aaron. Six participants receive one piece of paper apiece. Each participant must tell what is written on the paper to one of the group members in a gossipy fashion, and to another one in a non-gossipy fashion.
   1. I was at Aaron's house and the house was very dirty.
   2. Aaron failed his math test.
   3. Aaron stopped going out with Eve.
   4. Aaron has a retarded brother.
   5. Aaron's father has another new car.
   6. Aaron is thinking about going to a different school next year.

6) Three different participants volunteer to play Aaron, the boy about whom everyone is talking. They express how they felt when these things were being said about them in a gossipy way; what hurt them and what didn't.

7) Hold a brief discussion about the following points:
   — How did I feel about passing information along?
   — How did I feel as a "gossip"?
   — How did I feel listening to gossip?
   — How did I feel listening to information?
   — How would you suggest that Aaron deal with the gossip?
   — a. Is anyone ready to relate something from his personal experience about encountering and being hurt by gossip?
     b. How did you cope with it?
     c. How would you cope today, in the light of the group experience?

* It is not possible to ignore the differences that are possible between the understanding of the concept of gossip among boys and among girls. However, it is important to avoid going off on a tangent about the differences between boys and girls in general. Therefore, it is recommended to put question two first and then concentrate more fully on question one.

* It is possible to illustrate this with a role-play.

    d. What do others in the group suggest?

The answer to the last question will be considered the conclusion of the activity.

9. Revealing Secrets

Process:

1) The participants are divided into three groups. Each group gets a piece of paper with a topic on it.

TOPICS
1. I have found out that my friend talked about me to other friends.
2. I told a family secret to my friend and then found out that he told it to some others.
3. I heard that my friend made a lot of accusations about me to some other friends.

Each participant writes down for himself:
What I felt (at the time it happened)...
What I wanted to do (at the time it happened)...

2) The participants in each group collect the reactions and write them with a black magic marker on a large piece of posterboard in two columns:

* We are intending three separate circumstances, one for each group, where none of the groups are aware what is the topic for the other groups.

* The facilitator prepares three packets of notes (containing enough for one per member of the group). On each note is written the topic and the questions: "what did I feel?" and "what did I want to do?"

The Topic	
What I felt:	What I wanted to do:

3) The facilitator hangs the posterboard from each group on the board and compares the answers in the following way:
   — Sensitivities aroused in the three examples (first column)
   — Responses suggested by the three examples (second column)
   — What would each response lead to?

4) The facilitator asks the participants who are willing to tell personal experiences having to do with revealing secrets or unfounded accusations; how they felt and how they dealt with them.
5) Hold a brief discussion according to the following points:
   — What is the difference between natural curiosity which leads us to talk about others and talking the purpose of which is to cause dissension and damage? (relate examples)
   — Should you never ever tell secrets? (relate examples)

* It is possible to emphasize the difference between telling secrets in order to help (even in secret) and telling secrets in order to spread rumors or blacken someone's reputation. The next part illustrates the issue of helping or crisis intervention even at the price of revealing secrets. It is suggested to read the story like a play and hand out roles, and then discuss the question at the end.

Butting In

Denise: Have you noticed that Al's mood has been really rotten lately? He's been getting lousy grades too and he hasn't come to one of our get-togethers and has really been missing out. I live next door and I know that he is having a lot of trouble with his parents. His mother is sick and his father fights with him and with the rest of the family and is forcing him to get a job and doesn't let him do his homework or get ready for tests and he has to watch his brothers as well as work after school.

Mike: So, why doesn't he say anything? Do the teachers know?

Denise: That's the point! Al is hiding everything! He doesn't want anyone to know his business. He is shy or is afraid that people will feel sorry for him. Remember that he didn't come to our last party?

Jack: Sure! He was sick, wasn't he? You told us yourself.

Denise: I did not. I saw him that very morning. He was just fine. But he made me swear not to say anything. His father wouldn't give him permission to go and didn't want to give him any money so that he could join us. Al absolutely would not let me tell you guys anything. I didn't and it really bothers me. I don't know, but maybe even though he feels that way, we ought to butt in?

Mike: But if it's so important to him that we shouldn't know anything, wouldn't it hurt him even more if we butt in?
If he really wanted us to help him, wholdn't he say so?

Denise: I really don't know. Maybe he'll never

> his self-esteem depends on you not knowing. What should we do?
> How would you answer Denise?

— Is what "we'd like to do" in circumstances like the ones shown in the exercises the most effective coping strategy or not? Why?
— What would I feel impelled to do in response to the circumstances portrayed?
— Are other ways to respond which I might like to suggest?
— What have we learned from the experience of changing roles, both in terms of feeling and in terms of coping strategies?

10. Insults, Competition and Jealousy

Process:
1) The facilitator begins:
   "Today we will also deal with different kinds of conflicts which occur in friendship."

   The participants are divided into four groups. Each group gets the descriptions of two circumstances and relates to the concluding questions. These are the circumstances:

CIRCUMSTANCES

GROUP A & C:
Circumstance No. 1

> My friend Evan usually comes to school without having done any homework and always copies mine. One day I forgot my geography homework at home and I asked him to give me his to copy. Evan refused by saying:

What did Evan say?
What did I feel?
What do I intend to do or say?

Circumstance No. 2

> Gary asks me to do some (school) work for him. Usually, I don't mind doing something like that, but if I give in to his request, I won't be able to finish my homework. I don't want him to think that I don't want to help him...

What do I say to Gary?
How do you think Gary will respond?
Concluding Questions:
1. What is the central problem raised by the situations?
2. What would be effective ways to deal with problems of this sort?
2) Each group presents the circumstances, the questions and the coping suggestions to the entire group.
3) Hold a brief discussion covering the following points:
   — What was the central problem raised by each group?
   — What coping strategies were suggested in each case?
   — Are there additional suggestions?
   — Did participants relate personal experience with similar situations, what happened and how they dealt with it?

— Did the group suggest alternative coping strategies?

The discussion concludes the exercise.

GROUP B & D:
Circumstance No. 1

> Rachel tells: "Rose is the most popular girl in my class. Yesterday I told her a secret about my best friend Leslie so that she would be my friend."

Why is it important to Rachel to be friends with Rose? How will Leslie react when she finds out about what Rachel has done? What will Rachel say to her?

Circumstance No. 2

> Ron: Don, did you hear? Saturday night there is going to be a big party over at Gerry's. Are you coming?

Don: No, I wasn't invited...

What did Don feel?
What did Ron feel?
How will Ron react?

Concluding Questions:
1. What is the central problem raised by these situations?
2. What are the most effective ways of coping with problems of this sort?

11. The Third One in a Friendship Group

Process:
1) The facilitator opens:
   "Sometimes a third person appears in a friendship made up of two. How does this factor affect the relationship between the friends? Today, let's deal with this problem."
   The participants are divided into four groups. Each group gets a card with a circumstance on it and relates to the questions written at the end. The circumstances are described below:

* Two types of circumstances are presented: the entry of a person of the same sex to the friendship group and the entry of a person of the opposite sex. Each type is presented for each sex.
* When the groups are working on analyzing the circumstances, the facilitator should pick two girls who act well and give them the story line for "Phyllis and Sally" so that they can plan to present it as a play for the whole group right after the sub-group discussions are finished and before the final conclusions.

CIRCUMSTANCES
Group A & B:

> Debby and Amy are good friends. In the past they have helped each other, they understand one another and spend a lot of time together. Lately, Debby has been going around with Lena. Sometimes she asks Amy to join them, but most of the time Amy says no.

Amy feels that... Debby feels that... Amy would like to do (or say) ... How would Amy behave in Debby's place?

Group C & D:

> Ian and Brian are good friends who spend a lot of time together. Recently Ian met Susan and they have started going out together. As a result Ian has not been able to spend as much time with Brian as before.

What does Brian feel?
What does Ian feel?
How would Brian behave in Ian's place?

2) The participants rejoin the entire group.
   The facilitator says:
   "Before we discuss the significance of these circumstances and what the groups have raised, let's look at another illustration of a similar circumstance."
   Two girls present the situation, "Phyllis and Sally" as follows.
   The facilitator or one of the group members reads the details of the background for the situation:
   "We have here in front of us two very good friends: Phyllis and Sally. Their friendship was so strong and deep that they never got involved with other boys or girls. Two weeks ago Sally met Randy, a boy from a different class. As a result of her new friendship with Randy, she has cancelled get-togethers with Phyllis several times. On the day of the event, the two had agreed to meet at Phyllis' house in the evening."

   Phyllis
   Straightens up the room. Prepares refreshments and waits for Sally. She talks a little to herself, about how happy she is that Sally is finally coming over and they can chatter and gossip etc.
   She begins to look nervously at her watch, it is getting later and Sally is late.
   Finally, the telephone rings: Sally is cancelling out.
   Phyllis says: "Fine."

She says to herself: "Boy! I should have expected something like this. Here I went to such trouble and I prepared and I was so happy, it's really disappointing. What's going on with Sally? How she has changed!"

Sally
Getting dressed up, putting on make-up, putting on jewelry, looking at herself over and over in the mirror. Suddenly she remembers that she had promised Phyllis to come over to her house at the same time she had a date with Randy. Sally calls Phyllis on the phone: "Phyl, please forgive me but I totally forgot that I promised to come over tonight and, well, Randy already got tickets for a movie and he'll be here in about two minutes to pick me up. I am really sorry, but it's really so late now and we'll see each other tomorrow in school. Okay?"
Sally hears Phyllis' answer and says to herself: "It's really great to have a friend like Phyllis who is so understanding..." .

Notes
It's a good idea to have some props to help in creating a good atmosphere, like: a plate of refreshments, a toy telephone, a tablecloth, a mirror, cosmetics, a watch, etc.

3) After the play, "Phyllis and Sally" the facilitator asks for some volunteers in the group to play the meeting between Phyllis and Sally meeting the next day in school.

4) A discussion is held according to the following points:
   — What do Phyllis and Sally feel and think?
   — What do the other images, from the previous circumstances, feel? (a representative from each group can recount the circumstances and the conclusions of the group to the entire group)
   — What needs are being expressed by these images?
   — Are there any differences between boys and girls, in needs, feelings or coping strategies?
   — Does anyone want to tell about personal experiences which are similar, how he felt and how he coped?
   — The group may suggest additional alternate solutions

General Summation for the Exercises on Conflicts in Friendship

Friends get caught up in different situations during the period of their friendship. These situations arise out of different needs, out of a difference in developmental rhythm, out of different expectations and so on. Therefore, there is a need for discussion among friends and the candid expression of feelings (even negative feelings). Similarly, there is a need for understanding, that each one has a right to be interested in different things and to have friends in addition to those things which they share with their regular friends, without lessening the value of their first friendship or damaging it.

12. Anger and Ending Friendship

Aims:
* Legitimizing "negative" feelings (anger, hostility, etc.) which arise from time to time within friendship
* Practicing different ways of dealing with "negative" feelings by seeing the dispute from different points of view
* Awareness of the different reasons for wishing to continue or wind up a friendship
* Understanding that ending a friendship is a way of resolving a conflict so as to enable bringing the relationship to its natural conclusion without feeling guilty
* Learning different ways of ending a friendship

Process:
1) The facilitator says:
   "Sometimes it happens that we feel angry at a friend. Let's take a look at the following question: When I am really angry, what do I do?" Go around the group and relate to the question.
2) The facilitator says:
   "We have seen that people have different ways of reacting to angry feelings. Let's get into the subject a bit more deeply."
   The participants are divided into groups of four or five members each. Each one tells the other members of the subgroup about something which happened when he became angry at a friend and about what he did. Similarly, he tells how he felt about his reaction to his own anger-if he was satisfied, if he regretted anything, if he would react differently now, etc. The other members of the subgroup support him in his response or suggest other ways of reacting.

3) One of the participants volunteers to tell the entire group about a circumstance in which he became angry at a friend, reacted and was not happy with his reaction. Two participants volunteer to act out the situation with different reactions. Afterwards, the players switch roles so that each one has a chance to practice from both points of view.

* Other participants are invited to present different responses.
* It is possible to repeat the process and bring up other circumstances if the members of the group initiate further examples of characteristics which have angered them.

4) Hold a discussion covering the following points:
— Is it natural to feel anger, even hatred at times, towards a friend?
— What do I feel when my friends express anger or hatred towards me?
— Is a fight a good way to deal with anger?
— How did each of the participants feel in the role-play when they expressed anger towards a friend and when the friend expressed anger towards them?
— How is it possible to express anger towards a friend without hurting him?

* The point is to describe different ways of expressing the feelings and the behavior without hurting the friend, neither physically (beating him up) nor emotionally (insulting him), etc.

— When you wish to preserve a friendship, is the same reaction to anger appropriate for different friends? Who can tell about examples of this?

* The point is to consider the character of the friend and examine to what degree a certain reaction, like yelling, is appropriate or if it would destroy the friendship.

— Often we broadcast a "double message" to a friend: we say, for example "I am so disappointed that I have nothing more to say to you." but we really want to continue our friendship.
How can we make our real intentions clear?

* It is important to emphasize this point. It is possible to say, for example, "I am really very angry, disappointed, etc. But our friendship is also really important to me." or "That really hurt me a lot, but let's see how we can deal with the problem together."

Interim Summation

We have seen that each one gets angry at friends sometimes and that this is natural. There are different ways of reacting to angry feelings and it is important that everyone learns how to deal with those feelings and considers the friend's point of view.

5) The facilitator says:
   "Sometimes as a result of getting angry with a friend, you begin to want to end the friendship. There may be other reasons to end a friendship. Let's consider these two questions in a brief round of discussion:
   1. Is it okay to want to end a friendship?
   2. What else besides anger could be possible reasons for wanting to end the friendship?"

* The point is feeling the endpoint of the relationship; a difference in needs or interests; a difference in developmental rate; a feeling that whatever was acceptable was no longer significant, etc.

6) The facilitator says:
   "We have seen that there are different reasons for wanting to end a friendship and there is no reason to feel guilty about it. The question before us now is-how to do it."
   The facilitator asks one of the willing participants to show the group, in a role-play, how he would end a friendship.
   The participant decides if he wishes to include the friend with whom he concluded his friendship in order to show how he reacted and develops a dialogue between them; or he tells about the conclusion to his friendship with a third party and someone acts out the part of the third party; or he prefers to tell the group how he concluded his friendship as it appeared to him. Afterwards the facilitator asks one or more of the participants to

enter into the role-play and say: "If I were your friend, I would have felt...."
7) Repeat the process with additional participants, bringing up different reasons for and additional ways of ending friendships.

* The facilitator should focus on different ways of concluding the relationships.
It is important to relate to the feeling of what is "enough friendship" as well as to the feeling of wanting to end the friendship process.

8) Hold a brief summation in which the participants relate to the following points:
   — What have we gotten out of the meeting?
   — Why is it important to learn how to end friendships?

   Conclusion
   We have seen that there are different ways to end a friendship. Each one must choose the way that is right for him while considering the needs of the friend as well as his personality.

13. Loneliness

Aims:
* Strengthening awareness of loneliness-theirs and that of others
* Recognizing a situation of loneliness by design
* Learning different ways of coping with loneliness as a problem

Process
1) The facilitator begins by saying:
   "In our meetings we have been talking about friendship and have taken for granted that we all have friends all the time. That is not always the case. Sometimes we feel lonely or see that others

are lonely. Today let's deal with our own feelings of loneliness as well as with those of others."

Each participant receives a piece of paper (see below) and marks each statement: I agree/I disagree.

STATEMENTS ABOUT LONELINESS

1.	Being lonely means being by yourself.	Agree	Disagree
2.	It's not natural or healthy to be alone.	Agree	Disagree
3.	It's terrible to stay home alone on Saturday night; it's important to get out at all cost.	Agree	Disagree
4.	Everyone needs some time to be by himself.	Agree	Disagree
5.	Better to stay by yourself than to be with someone you don't really like.	Agree	Disagree
6.	An exercise in "Being Alone" would contribute a great deal to one's development and maturity.	Agree	Disagree
7.	Sometimes a person feels lonely even when he is surrounded by other people	Agree	Disagree

2) Hold a brief round of discussion in which the participants can express their reactions to the statements.

* This exercise is aimed at creating motivation to deal with the subject. Therefore it is not recommended to have a general discussion to extract ideas from the statements, but rather to simply briefly summarize the feelings of the members of the group.

3) In order to illustrate that "being alone" is not "being lonely" and to get more deeply into the subject, it would be advisable to show a film.
4) After the film, a discussion is held on the following points:
   — What is loneliness?
   — What feelings does it awaken?
   — What are the effects of loneliness?
5) The facilitator asks the participants to tell a personal experience about loneliness-either about themselves or about someone they know.

In conclusion the facilitator says:
"We have seen that each one of us feels lonely from time to time. There are different ways to deal with loneliness, either on our own or with the help of others. That is what we will talk about the next time we get together."

14. Making New Friends

Aim:
Learning different ways to make new friends.

Process:
1) The participants are divided into four groups. Each group gets an account of one of four circumstances and relates to the questions.

CIRCUMSTANCE NO. 1

Part of an Interview with Roger:
"...I have been fighting with my best friend for years. I got so angry with him I finally decided I had had enough. Now I am realizing that without him I don't have any good friends at all, since we were always together. So now I am lonely and I don't know what to do..."

Questions for discussion:
1. What would everyone have felt had they been Roger?
2. How can we help Roger? (It is important that the suggestions be detailed and not general. For example, I would do.... or I would have said.....)

CIRCUMSTANCE NO. 2

> Part of an interview with Sharon:
> "...Today, like usual, I didn't stand around in the schoolyard after school. I wanted to talk with someone but everyone was walking in small groups and it seemed to me that they wanted to stay away from me. Over the years I have felt that the other kids at school and in my neighborhood were not interested in being friends with me. I don't really understand why they stay away. I ask myself why am I so different? Why doesn't this happen to someone else? It really bothers me. I feel very hurt. I've gotten used to being by myself, but it still hurts that they don't ask me to join in...."

Question for discussion:
1. What would everyone have felt had they been Sharon?
2. How is it possible to help Sharon? (It is important that the suggestions be detailed and not general. For example, "I would have put my arms on her shoulder and said...."

2) A representative of each group reports about the circumstance and the responses that were given to the entire group.

3) Hold a discussion with the entire group about the following points:
   — In what ways is it possible to help those who feel lonely?
   — Is there a difference between how girls and boys relate to the topic of loneliness?
   — Why do people prefer to be alone sometimes?
   — What is the "price" that people pay for the wish to be alone?
   — In what ways can the participants help themselves when they feel lonely?
   — What does the phrase: "make friends with" signify?

* The facilitator should encourage the participants to bring up examples from their own experience or from that of acquaintances-for each of the points of discussion. It is possible to use these examples for role-play or exchange of roles especially to increase coping with loneliness.
* The emphasis in the final point is on the active quality of making friends.

15. Accepting Differences within Friendship

Aim:
Learning to accept being different within the friendship

Process:
1) The facilitator begins:
   "In the last meeting we dealt with the subject of loneliness-both by choice and not. Sometimes when someone is "different" he is forced to be lonely. Today, let's deal with this topic."
2) Hold a brief round of discussion in which the participants can suggest different ways of helping an isolated youth to become integrated into the group.
3) The participants are divided into groups of 4-5 members. Each group discusses and agrees upon ways that they help an isolated youth help himself make friends.

4) Each group presents their conclusions before the entire group. The facilitator chooses several ways which have been suggested and asks the participants to act them out in a role-play.

16. Concluding Meeting

To conclude the work on the subject of friendship, we have suggested several possibilities from which the facilitator can choose options which he feels are appropriate for his group.

Possibility A
Each participant is asked to bring something to the last meeting which will express the significance of friendship for him today (a thing, a song, a poem, a picture, a proverb, etc.).
In the meeting the participants will show everyone the things which they have brought and tell the reasons for choosing them, what they signify and about all the doubts they had before they made their choice.
The participants will share their feelings with the others in the group and will tell what they got out of the unit on friendship, in what way(s) they have made progress in the subject (they should relate examples) and what they would like to do to apply what they learned in the future.

To Conclude: what have we gotten out of dealing with "friendship"?

Possibility B:

The facilitator asks the participants to answer the questionnaire "What are my expectations of a friend?"

The participants are divided into groups. Each group considers the qualities important to friendship according to the results of their filling out the questionnaire. They then summarize them according to the template below:

Important qualities:	
Unimportant qualities:	
Qualities about which one can compromise:	

The content of each group's templates is presented to the entire group and a brief comparison is made. The participants who are willing tell if there has been any change in the way they have related to their friends and should use examples.

How I feel in the group.

When you are in a social group, to what degree, in your opinion, do you feel comfortable about doing the following things. Please circle the number which represents your reaction to each sentence: 1 = I feel very uncomfortable, 2 = I feel pretty uncomfortable, 3 = I feel pretty comfortable, 4 = I feel very comfortable.

		I feel very uncomfortable	I feel pretty uncomfortable	I feel pretty comfortable	I feel very comfortable
1.	Say I am glad to meet someone	1	2	3	4
2.	Agree with the opinions and feelings of one of the group members	1	2	3	4
3.	Encourage one of the group members to finish telling about an idea of his	1	2	3	4
4.	Ask one of the group members to explain what he just said	1	2	3	4
5.	Ask one of the group members to say what he thinks about different things	1	2	3	4
6.	Ask one of the group members to talk about himself	1	2	3	4
7.	Suggest things to the group	1	2	3	4
8.	Express my personal opinion	1	2	3	4
9.	Summarize what someone else in the group has said	1	2	3	4
10.	Say that I disagree with something someone in the group has said	1	2	3	4

	I feel very uncomfortable	I feel pretty uncomfortable	I feel pretty comfortable	I feel very comfortable
11. Express justified criticism of someone in the group	1	2	3	4
12. Disagree with the facilitator	1	2	3	4
13. Talk about my feelings in front of the group				
14. Share a personal experience with the group	1	2	3	4

What are my expectations of a friend

How important are the following things in your relationship with a good friend? Circle the number which most nearly represents your feeling: where 7 = very important, 6 = important, 5 = pretty important, 4 = important and unimportant to the same degree, 3 = not so important, 2 = not important and 1 = not at all important

1. You would never disappoint one another	1	2	3	4	5	6	7
2. You each would have other friends	1	2	3	4	5	6	7
3. You would never fight	1	2	3	4	5	6	7
4. If there is ever a misunderstanding, you would be able to talk about it	1	2	3	4	5	6	7
5. Each of you knows what the other expects	1	2	3	4	5	6	7
6. You would never make friends with someone the other wouldn't like	1	2	3	4	5	6	7
7. Your friendship would help develop your personality	1	2	3	4	5	6	7
8. A true friend would accept your craziness	1	2	3	4	5	6	7
9. Your friendship will last for years	1	2	3	4	5	6	7
10. Each of you will have time for yourself	1	2	3	4	5	6	7
11. If one of you heard accusations against the other, he would always rise to defend the other	1	2	3	4	5	6	7
12. You would be together all the time	1	2	3	4	5	6	7

13. You would have the same hobbies and interests	1	2	3	4	5	6	7
14. You would know how to wind up the friendship when there'd be no more point to it	1	2	3	4	5	6	7
15. A true friend would never make you angry	1	2	3	4	5	6	7
16. You would never be jealous of each other	1	2	3	4	5	6	7
17. You wouldn't have secrets from each other	1	2	3	4	5	6	7
18. You would help each other cope with problems	1	2	3	4	5	6	7
19. Even if you felt like being alone, you would agree to stay with the other if the other needed you	1	2	3	4	5	6	7
20. You would like to do homework together	1	2	3	4	5	6	7
21. You enjoy various activities even when you are not doing them together	1	2	3	4	5	6	7